SOUTH

THE RACE TO THE POLE

SOUTH

THE RACE TO THE POLE

EDITED BY PIETER VAN DER MERWE WITH JEREMY MICHELL

CONWAY

LONDON · OXFORD · NEW YORK · NEW DELHI · SYDNEY

NATIONAL
MARITIME MUSEUM
GREENWICH

CONWAY

Bloomsbury Publishing Plc
50 Bedford Square,
London, WC1B 3DP, UK

BLOOMSBURY, CONWAY and the Conway logo are trademarks
of Bloomsbury Publishing Plc

First published in Great Britain 2018
This edition published 2018

A catalogue record for this book is available from the British Library.
Library of Congress Cataloguing-in-Publication data has been applied for.

ISBN: PB: 978-1-8448-6486-7; ePDF: 978-1-8448-6484-3; ePub: 978-1-8448-6483-6

2 4 6 8 10 9 7 5 3 1

Design by Nicola Liddiard, Nimbus Design
Printed in China by RRD Asia Printing Solutions Limited

Acknowledgements

John Shears, British Antarctic Survey; Kåre Berg, Director, Fram Museum, Oslo; Jacqui McLeod; Jane Ace, Tina Warner, Harvey Edser, Ken Hickey, Alasdair Macleod, Rob Petherick, National Maritime Museum; Ann Savours Shirley, polar expert and former Keeper of Manuscripts, National Maritime Museum; Per Olav Torgnesskar, Assistant Curator, National Library of Norway, Oslo Division, Picture Collection; Gerard A. Sellek, Department of Chemical Engineering, University of Bath; Max Jones, University of Cambridge; Philippa Smith, Scott Polar Research Institute, University of Cambridge; David E. Yelverton, Fellow of the Royal Geographical Society; Linda Zealey, Foreign and Commonwealth Office, London.

CONTENTS

DIRECTOR'S FOREWORD

In January 1773, on his second Pacific voyage, Captain Cook was the first to cross the Antarctic Circle in search of a long-imagined 'great southern continent', only eventually to be blocked by impenetrable ice in latitude 71° south. Although he did not know it, he was then already well within the northern sweep of Antarctica's long peninsular arm, stretching out towards South America. It was only from the 1830s that commercial whalers, sealers, and then naval explorers slowly began to sketch in points and stretches of the Antarctic coast, thereby initiating the second act of a 'heroic age' of polar exploration that would last until the First World War. Cook aside, the curtain only really rose after the defeat of Napoleon in 1815, with the systematic and largely Royal Naval quest for a North-West Passage from the Atlantic to the Pacific. This was eventually found as a by-product of the many searches for Sir John Franklin's lost 1845 expedition, but the discovery was of little value save the honour, as the route was unnavigable for practical purposes.

By 1876, the Navy also demonstrated that the North Pole could not be reached by sea and main attention thereafter turned south. This followed some earlier work there and the commercial whalers and sealers who had already done so after largely exhausting traditional Arctic grounds. Such interests demanded better charting and scientific investigation of the Southern Ocean, where the slow revelation of an icy and uninhabited new continent with demonstrably rich natural resources offshore – and who knew what onshore – went hand-in-hand with early territorial claims upon it. These investigations, claims and rivalries led to the 'race to the South Pole' and the first attempt at a trans-Antarctic crossing in 1914 just as the First World War began. From a British cultural perspective, both became high points in the proud national tradition of heroic failure, and the superior merit of 'playing the game' rather than winning. It was Amundsen, an original-thinking Norwegian, who eventually won the race to the Pole. Captain Scott, a Royal Naval officer trying to fulfil Imperial expectations by traditional British methods, died bravely losing it, while Ernest Shackleton, another 'outsider' in conventional terms, turned the failure of his trans-continental attempt into a triumph of both team survival and what is still regarded as exemplary modern leadership.

This is the story told here in an extended and more generously illustrated second edition of a book we first published in 2000. The new edition showcases the Museum's extensive Polar collections, ranging from prints, paintings, ships' plans and photographs to personal items, polar and navigational equipment. It is one among several publications that accompany the new 'Polar Worlds' gallery – including both north and south polar exploration – which forms part of the new Exploration Wing opening at the National Maritime Museum in 2018. We are grateful to Pieter van der Merwe for his work on both editions, to the other original contributors, and to Jeremy Michell, Curator of Ship Plans and Historic Photographs, for his expansion of the final chapter carrying the story forward from its earlier ending with the deaths of Amundsen and Shackleton in the 1920s and for undertaking the picture research and captions.

Much has altered in Antarctica even since 2000. Scientific studies, especially relating to the effects of climate change, are ever more regularly reported from the many permanent research stations now long-established there. It continues to be a destination for those seeking personal challenges and also one with expanding leisure appeal in the form of specialist cruises. Among its attractions are the 'historic' buildings, sites and abandoned relics of the 'heroic age' of its first exploration, a material heritage now under wide and active conservation.

On behalf of everyone at the Museum, I hope you enjoy this book and I welcome you to discover more exciting stories in the 'Polar Worlds' gallery told through items in our collection.

Dr Kevin Fewster, AM, Director, Royal Museums Greenwich

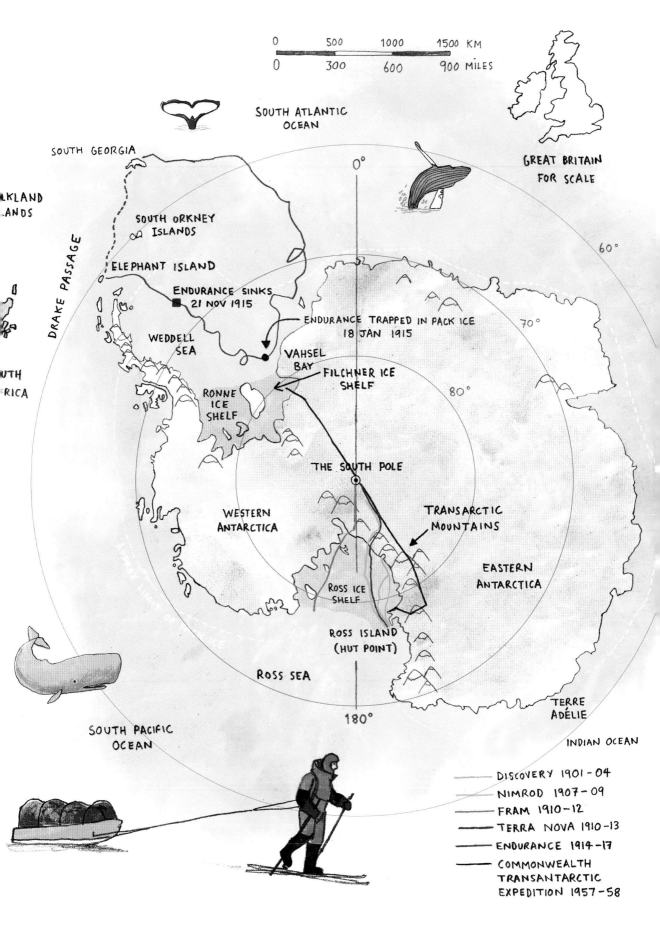

Looking up the Gateway to the Beardmore Glacier with Mount Hope on the left; taken by Captain R. F. Scott, 9 December 1911.

WHITE DESERT

by Pieter van der Merwe

Most people know the Moon better than Antarctica. The ice-bound continent at the far end of the world is the fifth largest, Europe and Australasia being smaller, but until the early 1800s it was as far beyond human imagination as it is beyond sight.

Antarctica's 14.2 million km² (5.5 million square miles) would cover the United States and Central America, while France and Britain together would fit easily into either of its two great bays, the Ross and Weddell Seas. Apart from small areas of the coastline and the peaks of its mountain ranges, it is permanently covered by some 29 million km³ (7 million cubic miles) of ice, lying on average between just under 2 and just over 3.6km thick (1.25–2.25 miles). The ice sheet has been there for at least 25 million years. Its weight is so vast that, in places, it has pressed the underlying land mass hundreds of metres below sea level.

> *Great God, this is an awful place*
>
> Scott at the South Pole, 17 January 1912

Over 90 per cent of the world's fresh water is locked up in the Antarctic ice. Were it to melt, the planet would become uninhabitable and its land would shrink unrecognisably as the oceans rose by between 45 and 60 metres (150–200 feet), drowning most of the islands and coastal nations that we know. Of New York, London and other great maritime cities, only the abandoned shells of tall buildings would rise above the surface. Seen from these decaying grave markers, the view would often be of many new islands but with extensive land only on distant horizons, if visible at all.

Antarctica would also look very different but would still be the size of Australia and Indonesia. The peaks of the great Transantarctic Mountains would rise to between 2,000 and 4,000 metres (6,500–13,000 feet) over the rocky plateau of Eastern or Greater Antarctica. This is the older part of the continent, lying to the 'right' of the Greenwich and 180° meridians of longitude. Even below the ice this is still high ground, averaging about 460 metres (1,500 feet) above the sea. Western or Lesser Antarctica, the geologically younger area to the 'left' of longitudes 0/180°, which includes the 1,290km (800-mile) finger of the Antarctic Peninsula reaching towards South America, would by contrast have largely fragmented into an archipelago of islands between the enlarged Ross and Weddell Seas.

While the fossil record shows that prehistoric Antarctica was once a warm and life-rich zone, the prospect of a thaw making it one again is equally remote – man-made global warming aside. The ice and the rock beneath are inseparable and the continent is not only by far the coldest place on Earth but also the highest, the mean height of its frozen surface above the sea being between 2,130 and 2,440 metres (7,000–8,000 feet). This is more than twice as high as Asia, its nearest rival at 915 metres (3,000 feet) on average. The South Pole itself is at 2,900 metres (9,500 feet), so the European race to it was in no sense one between competitors and climate on a level playing field: it was a climb to, and endurance at, an altitude that is usually the province of mountaineers.

The spectacular grandeur of the West Antarctic Ice Sheet and mountains; taken from a window of a NASA 'Operation IceBridge' aircraft, 31 October 2016.

How the polar ice sheet originally formed is the subject of at least five theories. That it endures is partly due to its massive thermal inertia and altitude, and to the fact that the direct solar heat it receives during the brief Antarctic summer is reflected by its own whiteness into space rather than absorbed. Much also has to do with its being surrounded by the cold but biologically teeming waters of the Southern Ocean – the resource, in terms of whaling and sealing, that led to man's first commercial interest in the region in the 19th century.

Most remarkable, perhaps, is how little appears to sustain the mainland ice coverage. Antarctic cloud, drawn in from the warmer ocean to the north, is high and thin – another factor preventing heat retention. Rain is practically unknown save for occasionally on the coast, and snowfall is surprisingly light. On average, snow equivalent to only about 16.5cm (6.5 inches) of water falls in a year. Perhaps less than 5cm (2 inches) falls near the Pole, as the high-altitude cold air inland is about ten times drier than in temperate areas of the world. Very little melts, however, since most of the continent stays well below freezing. It is a vast, dry and intensely cold desert, built up layer on minute layer over unimaginable time. Nothing decays: mummified seals several thousand years old have been found well inland. One of Scott's dogs still guards his base camp nearly a century after its death, teeth bared in a desiccated snarl. Dead human bodies are preserved, freeze-dried, as is all normally biodegradable waste. The only indigenous plants are a scattering of highly adapted lichens and mosses clinging to exposed rock, mostly near the coast. All other life is sustained in or from the sea, with seals and penguins the only large animals that breed on the mainland.

In the deep Antarctic winter months of August and September, mean temperatures range from -20 to -30°C on the coast and from -40 to -70°C inland. In summer the interior remains between -20 and -35°C with the coast hovering around freezing point, although the Antarctic Peninsula can see brief rises to 15°C (59°F). By contrast, 0°C and -20 to -35°C are the normal summer and winter mean temperatures of the much warmer Arctic, which is a frozen ocean surrounded by continental land masses – it is Antarctica's complete physical as much as polar opposite. The lowest temperatures on Earth, -89.2°C (1983) on the high interior and -60°C near sea level, are Antarctic records. At such temperatures fuel oil congeals into jelly.

By far the worst aspect of the cold in human terms is the additional effect of 'wind chill', for every knot of wind speed is the physiological equivalent to a drop of one degree. Frostbite in such conditions is a routine danger and rapid hypothermic death a penalty for accidents or failures of planning. These are the hazards that Scott and Shackleton's generation were neither the first nor the last to face with no more than wool, silk and other natural types of clothing – none with the thermal efficiency of modern synthetics.

Wind is ever-present in Antarctica. The surrounding Southern Ocean is the stormiest in the world, with a 4.5-metre (15-foot) swell normal in calm conditions. Gales and cyclonic storms are perpetually being generated around the 'Antarctic Convergence' of cold polar air and seas with warmer ones at about latitude 50° south. These storms chase each other endlessly west to east around the world, creating huge seas that sweep on, unimpeded by intervening land save the few sub-Antarctic islands. The 'roaring forties' latitudes in which clippers like *Cutty Sark* drove eastwards on the Australian wool-run and home round Cape Horn merge with the 'filthy fifties', where the average wind speed is 37.7 knots – a force 8 gale. South from here, notwithstanding the wind, endemic Convergence fogs and the increased risks of ice add to hazards that only modern ships are fully equipped to handle.

> *If you drop a steel bar it is likely to shatter like glass, tin disintegrates into loose granules, mercury freezes into solid metal, and if you haul up a fish through a hole in the ice within five seconds it is frozen so solid that it has to be cut with a saw.'*
>
> John Bechervaise, *The Far South*, 1962

In the high mainland interior, winds are relatively light. However, heavy cold air pours down from the interior to the coast, creating fierce local storms. At worst, these 'katabatic' (descending) winds can average more than 160km/h (100 miles an hour) and have been measured in gusts of more than 240km/h (150 miles an hour). These storms easily become turbulent and, while no new snow is involved, they whip up the granular surface crystals formed by recent falls into lethal sub-zero blizzards. It was in such conditions on the low-lying Ross Ice Shelf that Scott's party died in 1912.

It is not only wind that pours off the highlands. So too, on a longer timescale, does the ice itself in the spectacular coastal glaciers that formed early explorers' gateways to the interior. Of these, the 161km (100-mile) Beardmore and the nearby Axel Heiberg Glaciers are (though not the largest) forever linked as Scott's and Amundsen's routes up to the Pole. They and five others flow down at a rate of about 335 metres (1,100 feet) a year to feed the Ross Ice Shelf, which fills the landward end of the Ross Sea. This – also called the Great Ice Barrier – is the largest of a dozen that make up about a third of the Antarctic coastline. At 803,000km² (310,000 square miles) it is larger than France, and ranges from 610 metres (2,000 feet) thick on the landward side to 185 metres (600 feet) thick at seaward.

The combined Filchner-Ronne Ice Shelf in the Weddell Sea – named after its German and American discoverers, Wilhelm Filchner (1911) and Finn Ronne (1947) – is next largest at about 451,000km² (174,000 square miles), of which the Ronne makes up just under 333,460km² (128,750 square miles). From the 'ice front' or outer edge of the shelves, which can present cliffs of more than 30 metres (100 feet) to approaching ships, tabletop icebergs more than a mile (over 1.5km) long routinely calve off and float more than 3,200km (2,000 miles) north before breaking up, which can take five years. They can be of even vaster size, 145km (90 miles) in one measured instance, and sometimes make spectacular appearances off the South African coast. This is an entirely normal process fuelled by pressure and stresses as mainland glaciers slowly push the shelves out from the coast, but it is also one that provides dramatic demonstrations of how global warming may be speeding up such mechanisms. Scientific opinion now agrees that the build-up of greenhouse gases, especially carbon dioxide, due to an ever-expanding human population's attrition on such carbon-sinks as rainforests and a still overwhelming reliance on fossil fuels, is warming the Earth's atmosphere and oceans at a debated but inexorable rate. Warming seas undoubtedly displace or destroy species and food chains that depend on cold waters and cannot rapidly adapt. They also change weather, usually for the worse in the short term and – should existing ocean currents also shift as a result – may produce radical and irreversible alterations of climate. Since 2000, there has been a dramatic and apparently permanent shrinkage of the Arctic ice cap, and while the Antarctic has far greater climatic inertia and stability from its greater area and (under the ice) an enormous land mass, it is also affected, albeit so far only at its outer edges. Whereas Arctic sea-ice depletion is largely from direct melting and that of the Greenland ice sheet is a 50/50 split between melting and icebergs, 99 per cent of Antarctic ice-sheet loss is from icebergs 'calving' from it. Even allowing that this is a peripheral process, a 2012 study predicted that the vast Filchner-Ronne Ice Shelf may largely disappear by the end of the 21st century, raising the world sea level by about 43cm (17 inches). In 1998 and 2010 two sections of it – nearly ten times the size of Greater London – broke off before disintegrating into smaller bergs, some of which were sighted 4,830km (3,000 miles) away off New Zealand. In 2000 the largest ever recorded, measuring just over 17, 600km^2 (6,800 square miles), detached from the Ross Sea Barrier, while in 2002 the 10,000-year-old Larsen-B ice-shelf in the Weddell area partially collapsed and is predicted to disappear entirely by about 2020. Most recently, in July 2017, and after creeping northwards for over ten years, a vast split in the Larsen-C shelf calved an iceberg – prosaically coded A68 – of about 5,800km^2 (2,240 square miles) – over three times the size of Greater London – with cliffs along the split over 457 metres (1,500 feet) high and an estimated mass of a trillion tons (i.e. 10^{12} or a million-million). Even this, however, comprises only 12 per cent of just the Larsen-C shelf. In January 2017, another crack developing in the Brunt Ice Shelf further east also forced the British Antarctic Survey to tow the 200-ton module comprising the current version of its Halley base, established in the 1950s, 23km (14 miles) further 'inland', to avoid the risk of being set adrift.

Scientific opinion now agrees that the build-up of greenhouse gases is warming the Earth's atmosphere and oceans at a debated but inexorable rate.

The degree to which these and other phenomena are either 'natural' or symptoms of climatic stress on a global scale due to human activity is much argued. But since neither air nor ocean respect human boundaries, the critical question is what the outcomes will be if they continue at an increasing rate. Apart from the huge costs of coastal protection, where practical, it will take little more than a metre of permanent global sea-level rise to drown some small, low-lying island states in the Pacific. This raises the question of where their people will go, or whether a nation can still exist if its land does not. Although likely to occur over long timescales and not as the result of the sort of sudden apocalypse envisioned by Hollywood disaster movies, the consequences of greater forced population shifts from large continental coastal areas, such as the Ganges delta, are even more incalculable. Other climate-change effects, like 'desertification' in parts of Africa, already contribute to more short-term causes of 'uncontrolled migration', but should rising seas drive coast-al-plain populations in the millions to compete for space and resources on already crowded higher ground and across political borders, currently familiar migration prob-

James Weddell with his ships reached a 'furthest south' in 1823 while seal-hunting and exploring in what became known as the Weddell Sea. Aquatint after WJ Huggins, October 1826.

lems may look quite minor. While there are climatic risks associated with Antarctica, it is a reassuring measure of its vast thermal inertia that – dramatic but peripheral symptoms like those mentioned aside – the last half-century of scientific readings across the continental interior has shown no significant long-term variation in its state of immemorial deep-freeze.

The main Antarctic Barrier ice and bergs are of fresh water, being formed originally from compacted snow. The seasonal pack ice, which is far more dynamic in its movement and covers the greatest area, forms by a complex process from seawater into sheets of up to about 15cm thick (6 inches), rising to about 1.8 metres (6 feet) or

A **1754 chart** of the southern Pacific, including an inset speculating about the size and shape of Antarctica, by Philippe Buache.

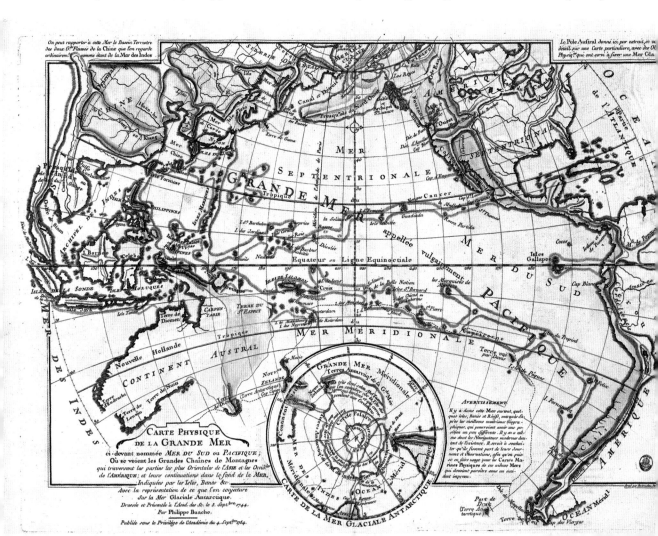

more if it survives for more than two years. By the time it has lasted three years it is 'old ice' and has lost its surface salinity, providing good drinking water. The mainland lies almost entirely within the Antarctic Circle (66° 33' south, the outer limit of 24-hour polar daylight in summer and darkness in winter) but the winter pack – at maximum extent in August and September – reaches north to latitude 54° in the Atlantic, 56–59° in the Indian Ocean sector and 60–63° in the Pacific, the Antarctic Convergence in both the last two being further south. At 60 nautical miles (112km) to each degree and expanding in all directions northwards, these are vast areas and can be greater in a severe season. Seen from space, the winter area of the Antarctic ice can practically double. However, there are astonishing variations, famously exemplified by the Scottish sealer James Weddell's penetration of the sea that bears his name in 1823, when he reached just over 74° south without encountering significant ice at all.

Linear distances are also daunting. The tip of the Peninsula is 965km (600 miles) south of Cape Horn across the stormy Drake Passage but, isolated islands apart, New Zealand is the next closest land at 3,380km (2,100 miles) away. South Africa is some 4,020km (2,500 miles) away and the south coast of Australia around 3,700km (2,300 miles). Lesser and Greater Antarctica together, measured west to east through the Transantarctic range, are about 4,500km (2,800 miles) across at their widest. The narrow land neck connecting them between the Ross and Weddell seas is under 965km (600 miles), excluding the ice shelves, which make the sea-to-sea distance far wider.

Looking south

Terra Australis recenter inventa sed nondum plene cognita. This optimistic Latin description, meaning 'Southern Land recently discovered but not yet fully known', first appeared on an imagined map of Antarctica in 1531. Its basis was twofold: a belief inherited from Classical times that an icy southern zone must exist to 'balance' the cold northern regions, and Magellan's passage in 1520 through the southern straits that now bear his name, during the first voyage round the world.

Captain James Cook's second voyage to the Pacific, 1772–1774, searched for a 'Southern Continent', reaching a furthest south of lat. 71° 10'. Painting by Nathaniel Dance, 1776.

This left the false impression that Tierra del Fuego was the tip of something much bigger. Somewhere in the preceding centuries the Classical notion of 'Terra Australis' being icy transformed into the idea that it was a more temperate 'counterweight' to northern lands and a potentially rich prize for its discoverers.

During the *Golden Hind*'s circumnavigation of 1577–1580, Francis Drake was driven well south of Cape Horn in 1578 into what is now the Drake Passage and clearly reported wide open seas and 'no maine or iland to be seen to the southwards'. However, neither this nor later southern island discoveries dislodged the myth of a temperate polar continent until the 1770s.

In that era of European commercial, colonial and finally ideological warfare, scientific navigation came into its own as a tool by which new lands could be found, fixed, claimed and drawn into an imperial embrace. Britain and France were the new contenders, with Spain defending a long-standing oceanic empire. In 1768–1770 Lieutenant James Cook's scientific *Endeavour* voyage to observe the transit of Venus across the Sun from Tahiti also charted New Zealand. The expedition proved that its two islands were no part of a polar continent, as Tasman had done for Australia in the early 1640s. With a recent history of both Spanish and French activity in southern latitudes, the government then decided to send Cook to resolve the 'Southern Continent' issue for good and, if it existed, claim it for Britain. Armed this time with a copy of John Harrison's newly perfected chronometer, to fix accurate longitude at sea, Cook's ships *Resolution* and *Adventure* spent the two antipodean summers of 1772–1774 pushing as far south as ice, fog, and endurance would allow.

It was the first modern Antarctic expedition. Cook approached from the Atlantic and Pacific, circumnavigating the continent without seeing it, though coming almost within sight at his most southerly point, latitude 71° 10', in 1773–1774. This latitude was not reached again in that area until 1959–1960. He returned with the first detailed account of pack ice and 'ice islands' (icebergs) and a belief that a cold land mass entirely within the 60th parallel south was their likely source. Based on his discovery of desolate South Georgia in 1775, he also said, with native Yorkshire pragmatism, that it might not be worth finding.

Cook died on Hawaii in 1779, with France already at war with Britain, and remaining so until 1783 as an ally of the American rebels. The French Revolutionary War began in 1793 and it was not until after Napoleon's defeat in 1815 that the Royal Navy began to think again of polar exploration. It had by then established a Hydrographic Office (in 1795) to make official charts and had a large number of underemployed younger officers seeking peacetime opportunities for glory. The period 1823–1854, with Francis Beaufort as Hydrographer (of the Beaufort Scale of wind speeds fame), proved to be one of great Royal Naval surveying. It was also one of Arctic exploration, as naval expeditions – the first in 1818 – revived the 16th-century quest for a North-West Passage around Canada,

Gathering fresh water from 'ice islands' (icebergs) in the South Atlantic on Cook's second voyage, 9 January 1773. Engraving after William Hodges, 1777.

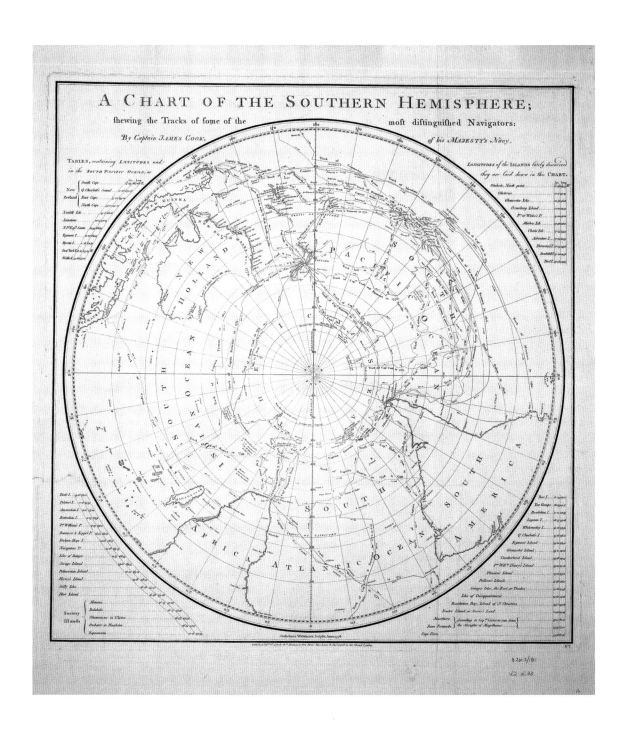

between the Atlantic and Pacific. From 1847 this effectively became a series of search parties (not all British or official) to discover the fate of Captain Sir John Franklin's 129-man expedition, which had left on the same quest in 1845 in Her Majesty's ships *Erebus* and *Terror*, and vanished without trace. The total loss of Franklin's party was only confirmed in 1859 and though in the process an ice-bound North-West Passage was found in 1850 by Robert McClure, it proved impassable to large sailing ships. Amundsen would be the first to sail through in the small *Gjøa* in 1903–1906. The last major Royal Naval Arctic expedition was one that tried to reach the North Pole by sea in 1875–1876 under Captain Sir George Nares, who had already seen Antarctic waters. Sledges attained 83° 20' north, but the Navy then rightly concluded there was no sea passage to the Pole and Arctic discovery was largely left to other nations and private interests.

There is some doubt on who first sighted the 'Antarctic continent', a phrase first speculatively used by Lieutenant Samuel Wilkes, who was commodore of a five-ship American naval expedition in 1838. The question, as Ross pointed out a few years later, was still 'is there a continent at all?' The two contenders are Lieutenant Thaddeus Bellingshausen of the Imperial Russian Navy, who went south in 1819–1821 with two ships and orders to make discoveries as close as possible to the Pole, and the British Royal Naval master Edward Bransfield. The disputed honour, by two days on 28 January 1820, may have been Bellingshausen's but he never made such a claim and his thorough work – which clarified what Cook had seen of the Antarctic islands, especially South Georgia and the South Sandwich group – was little noticed after his return.

At the same time commercial sealers, tipped off by Cook's reports, were already beginning to decimate the fur seal population from South Georgia to the South Shetlands. The latter were discovered in 1819 by William Smith, a British sealer, and Bransfield returned with him in January 1820, claiming them for Britain. On 30 January he sighted the tip of the Antarctic Peninsula, and he was certainly the first to chart part of the mainland. In 1822–1824 the sealer James Weddell found unusually open water far into what he called

Cook's chart of the southern hemisphere, published in 1777 after his second voyage. In contrast to Buache's 1754 chart (page 18), it shows his thoroughness in trying to locate a southern continent.

Captain James Clark Ross was a successful Arctic explorer before commanding a four-year Antarctic expedition, 1839–1843. Painting by John R Wildman, 1834.

the 'Sea of George IV' – now the Weddell Sea – but sealing became uneconomic in the 1830s and it was the whalers who made the next scientific contributions.

The most notable of many was the firm of Samuel Enderby and Son, based at Greenwich from 1834, who had opened up the British South Pacific whale fishery as far back as 1775. The Enderbys' was a successful concern, promoting discovery well beyond commercial justification because of their personal scientific interests. One of their captains, John Biscoe, circumnavigated Antarctica in 1831–1832 with the ships *Tula* and *Lively*, sighting and naming Enderby Land and further defining the west coast of the Peninsula, whose northern end he called Graham Land. Other Enderby discoveries followed but by the time of Queen Victoria's accession in 1837 a combination of scientific interest and the whaling potential had revived official involvement.

Over the next two years there were three naval expeditions in Antarctica: French, British and American. The first was under Captain Dumont d'Urville, and the second Captain Sir James Clark Ross, who had reached the North Magnetic Pole in 1831. Both aimed at finding the North Magnetic Pole's southern equivalent but were unsuccessful. (This was only first done in 1909, though not permanently, since the magnetic poles migrate.) Dumont D'Urville found the mainland coast in longitudes 120–160° east, naming it Terre Adélie after his wife and, more indirectly, its inhabitants – the Adélie penguins. Extraordinarily, he met but did not speak with the *Porpoise* of Samuel Wilkes's ill-equipped American Pacific expedition, which spent two difficult seasons investigating the southern whale fishery and also charted the coast now named after him.

Ross's hand-picked Royal Naval party of 1839–1841 and 1842–1843 was by contrast very well-found, sailing in two specially strengthened ships – *Erebus* and *Terror* – which were later to vanish with Franklin. Their first two seasons were the most productive, especially from January 1841 when Ross discovered and claimed the coast of what is now the Ross Dependency, with the Ross Sea and ice shelf (or 'Great Ice Barrier'). Here he named many of the features that were to become familiar in the saga of Scott and Amundsen. These included Possession Island, Cape Adare on the eastern side of the Ross Sea, the volcanoes Mounts Erebus and Terror on Ross Island (the former being active), and the sheltered McMurdo Sound, which lies between there and the mainland. Ross's discoveries made his Antarctic expedition the most important of the century and there is a strange irony in his ships' disappearance so soon afterwards in its greatest Arctic disaster.

Ross's success notwithstanding, the fragments of coast, ice and offshore islands so far discovered did not add up to proof of a single southern land mass. This remained the case until after the round-the-world oceanographic research voyage of HMS *Challenger,* under George Nares, in 1872–1876. *Challenger'*s brief foray into the Antarctic in 1874 was a minor part of her programme but she was the first steam vessel to cross the Antarctic Circle

HMS *Erebus* and *Terror* passing Beaufort Island and Mount Erebus, 28 January 1841. Later, Mt Erebus became the backdrop for the huts built by Scott and Shackleton. Watercolour by JE Davis, 1841.

HMS *Challenger* with icebergs in the background. Her Antarctic circumglobal expedition (1872–1876) laid the scientific foundations for future expeditions. Lithograph, 1 December 1880. ABOVE

One of the first photographs of Antarctic 'tabular' icebergs taken from HMS *Challenger* during her global scientific circumnavigation. Unknown photographer, February 1874. RIGHT

(66° 33' south) and while Nares did not see the mainland, the deep-sea geological samples he brought home proved to be of inland continental origin, dropped out to sea by ancient glacial movement.

During the next 20 years a few whalers went south into that region. The northern fishery was becoming exhausted, but with steam and the Norwegian Svend Foyn's invention of the harpoon gun revolutionising the industry, it looked southwards once again. On the east of the Antarctic Penin-sula the Larsen Ice Shelf commemorates the Norwegian

William Colbeck went to the Antarctic three times between 1898 and 1904. He flew his Pirate Yacht Club burgee when he, Borchgrevink and Savio reached a furthest south on 17 February 1900.

whaling captain who discovered much of the area and whose reports persuaded Foyn in 1894 to back a further voyage by Henrik Bull in the whaler *Antarctic*. On 24 January 1895, Bull and his men were the first to make a confirmed landing on the continent proper, near Cape Adare. One of them was a young Norwegian seaman and childhood friend of Amundsen called Carsten Borchgrevink. In 1898

The Belgian exploration ship *Belgica* trapped in the ice in the Bellingshausen Sea, where the crew were forced to overwinter in 1898. Photograph by FA Cook, 20 May 1898.

his so-called 'British Antarctic Expedition' was landed at Cape Adare from the whaler *Southern Cross*, to become the first to pass a winter on the mainland. Despite its name – required by its British sponsor, the publisher Sir George Newnes – Borchgrevink's party was largely Norwegian, and one of them died while ashore. When their ship collected them in January 1900, they briefly went further south. Here Borchgrevink, the English Lieutenant Colbeck and the Finnish dog handler Per Savio sledged 16km (10 miles) over the Ross Ice Shelf to 78° 50' south, the nearest to the Pole yet reached by man. The first ship to winter in the Antarctic – the *Belgica* under the Belgian Lieutenant Adrien de Gerlache – had then already done so too, but by accident. In 1898–1899 it was trapped for a year in the pack ice of the Bellingshausen Sea, west of the Antarctic Peninsula. This was a terrible experience for all concerned, including the Norwegian second mate, Roald Amundsen.

At the same time, money was being raised in London to launch what would be Scott's first expedition of 1901 in the *Discovery*. The moving spirit was Sir Clements Markham, President of the Royal Geographical Society since 1893, but as a former naval officer also a veteran of both the Franklin search (under Horatio Austin in HMS *Assistance*, 1850–1851) and Nares's Arctic voyage of 1875, on which his cousin Albert Hastings Markham was second-in-command and led the northward sledge party. He had come a long way since then, having left the Navy and, despite some difficulties, forged a successful career in what became the India Office. Here he was instrumental in starting quinine production in India, having organised transplantation of chinchona from Peru, and was loaned as geographer to a British punitive expedition in Ethiopia. A domineering and determined personality as well as a brilliant communicator, to whom the deeds of great explorers were meat and drink, Markham made a British Antarctic expedition the aim of his Presidency. His purpose was to widen geographical and scientific knowledge of the continent but, based on his own experience, he took it as axiomatic that the Royal Navy was the best organisation to undertake the task and that a naval officer should be the

He did not plan a race for the Pole but was also clear that Britain must get there first if contention arose.

Borchgrevink took 75 dogs with him to assist with pulling sledges as they explored the area. They were the first dogs used in Antarctica. Photograph by William Colbeck, 1900.

The huts at Camp Ridley, the first to be set up on the Antarctic continent, acted as a base for the sledging parties exploring the area. Photograph by William Colbeck, 1900.

Seals basking on newly-formed pancake ice off Cape Evans. The photograph was taken by H. G. Ponting, the Scott expedition's official photoghapher, c.1910. OPPOSITE

leader. He did not plan a race for the Pole but was also clear that Britain must get there first if contention arose.

Events spurred Markham on, including the 1895 Sixth International Geographical Conference in London, which placed priority on Antarctic discovery as 'the greatest piece of geographical exploration still to be undertaken'. It also rankled when Borchgrevink turned up fresh from Bull's expedition, addressing the Conference rather less than modestly about their first landing at Cape Adare in January and his own plans for what became the *Southern Cross* voyage. Markham tried to impede this but was frustrated by Newnes's sponsorship, which was all the more galling when his initial approaches for government support of his own plans were rebuffed.

From his Presidential chair, Markham nonetheless persuaded the Royal Geographical Society to put up £5,000 as seed corn for a public appeal and in early 1898 obtained the prestigious support of the Royal Society. The following year he found a wealthy business sponsor to add £25,000 to the £14,000 by then collected and finance was assured when the Treasury promised £40,000 in 'match-funding' to a similar private sum, which was already practically there.

What Markham now needed was a leader in his required mould. Walking home down the Buckingham Palace Road in June 1899, a chance encounter with someone he had first met more than ten years earlier resolved his problem.

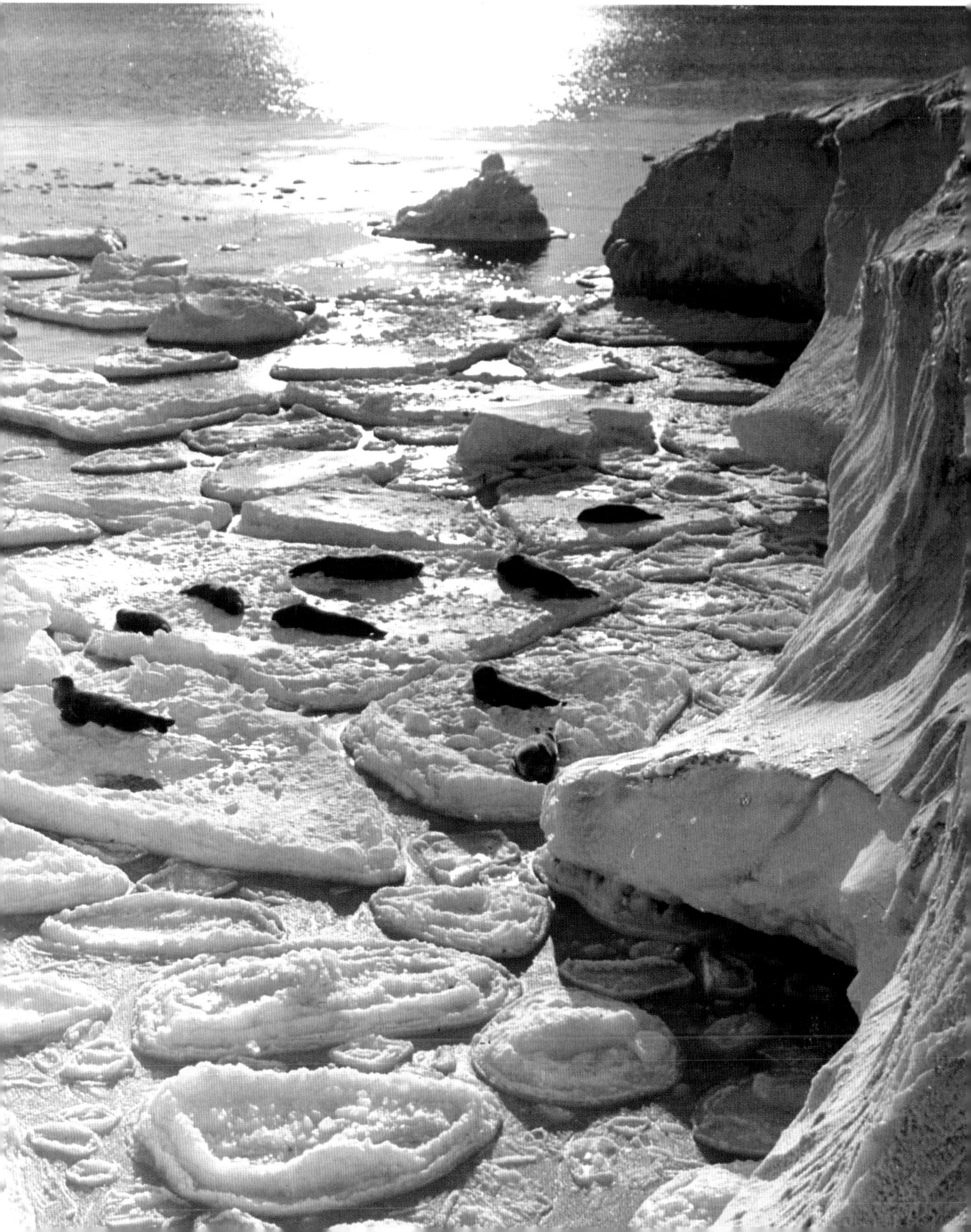

THE BALLAD OF THE SEAL & THE WHALE

I'll tell you a tale of a seal and a whale,
That lived in the far Southern sea.
The story they told to an Easterly gale,
The Easterly gale told to me.

In generic terms (I don't know who's to blame
For abusing these animals meek)
Leptonicotes Wedelli was the name
Of the seal: he'd object could he speak.

Now the whale had a name that would fill with
                                    surprise
A sage of the old-fashioned style.
Orca gladiator is a name that implies
A nature pugnacious and vile.

Before getting on with my yarn, I'll reveal
That Dame Nature her rule never bends.
For the Wedelli seal makes a very good meal
For the Orca, so they were not friends.

DISCOVERY AND NIMROD 2

by Pieter van der Merwe

Discovery, 1901–1904

[The Commander] must be a *naval officer* ... and he must be *young*. These are essentials. Such a commander should be a good *sailor* with some experience of ships under sail, a *navigator* with a knowledge of *surveying*, and he should be of a *scientific turn of mind*. He must have *imagination* and be capable of *enthusiasm*. His temperament must be *cool*, he must be *calm, yet quick* and *decisive* in action, *a man of resource, tactful* and *sympathetic*.

Sir Clements Markham

The man who crossed the road to greet Markham in 1899 was the torpedo lieutenant of the battleship *Majestic*, flagship of the Channel Squadron. It was within days of his 31st birthday and his name was Robert Falcon Scott. Known to his family as 'Con', Scott was born at Stoke Damerel, Devonport, on 6 June 1868, the third of six children and the elder of two sons. His parents both had naval connections, although his father, John, owned a Plymouth brewery. 'Con' was a rather dreamy, self-sufficient boy, largely educated at home until he went, relatively late, to board at a Hampshire preparatory school known for taking those intended for the Navy. He joined the training ship *Britannia* in 1881 and, despite minor scrapes, was made cadet captain early in 1883 before passing out seventh in a class of 26 that summer, with first-class certificates in mathematics and seamanship. He was still a midshipman in November 1886 when he joined the training ship *Rover*, which took him out to the West Indies. It was here that he first came to the notice of Markham by winning a cutter race. Markham invited Scott to dine with him in the squadron flagship, where the former was a guest of his cousin and fellow polar veteran, by now Admiral AH Markham. Markham was impressed by Scott's 'intelligence, information and the charm of his

Sir Clements Markham was a driving force behind the 1901 British Antarctic Expedition, and an advocate of man-hauling sledges based on his own previous Arctic experience. ABOVE

Robert Falcon Scott, shown here in full uniform with the Polar Medal from the 1901–1904 expedition. In the Navy he had specialised as a torpedo officer. Photograph by Maull & Fox, 1904-10.

manner', though Scott was not the only, or even the most favoured 'mid' to fall under his calculating eye.

Confirmed as a sub-lieutenant in 1888, Scott was posted to the cruiser *Amphion* in which he served in the Pacific and the Mediterranean, rising to lieutenant in 1889. Though he performed well, his letters at this time show he became depressed and dissatisfied both with the ship and himself, and probably realised that any prospect of command was a long way off. He thus changed course into the new and more specialised path of torpedo warfare, training at Portsmouth before returning to the Mediterranean late in 1893 as torpedo lieutenant of the *Vulcan*, an experimental vessel.

In the following autumn came the first of several family disasters. His father, John Scott, had some years before sold his brewery to retire in gentlemanly comfort but the money had been lost through poor investment. The large family home had to be let: Scott's younger brother, Archie, gave up his commission in the Royal Artillery and joined a local regiment in Nigeria where the pay was better and costs were less. The sisters all found work: the eldest, Ettie, to her mother's disquiet, became an actress but soon married a Member of Parliament. Their 63-year-old father resumed work as a Somerset brewery manager.

To be closer to home, Scott transferred to Portsmouth and in 1896 was serving in the *Empress of India* in the Channel Squadron when he met Markham again, this time a guest in the *Royal Sovereign* at Vigo when they were en route to Gibraltar. Now Sir Clements, Markham was renewing his campaign to mount a British Antarctic expedition following the Admiralty's initial refusal to assist. Scott heard little more of this campaign, though. Their ways quickly parted and the following year he transferred to the battleship *Majestic*.

Four months later, in July 1897, Scott's father died leaving just over £1,500, and the cost of supporting their mother fell largely to the two brothers. This tragedy and Scott's financial difficulties were compounded in 1898 when Archie also died, of typhoid, while on home leave. Scott now felt that he was burdened by ill fortune and that he had to find some way to advance himself more rapidly. It was in these circumstances that he met Markham in the street, heard that the National Antarctic Expedition seemed a real possibility, and two days later formally applied to command it. His success brought him promotion to commander, and in due course a further allowance.

It was nearly a year until Scott's appointment was confirmed by the Joint Committee of the Royal and Royal Geographical societies, of which Markham was vice-president. During this time Scott returned to *Majestic* under Captain Egerton, whose warm reference nonetheless pointed out that his junior had no knowledge of polar work. The same period also marked the successful end to a number of long-running battles for Markham, including getting his way that the prime aim of the voyage would be geographical rather than oceanographic and that the commander of the ship would also command the expedition, not a scientist. This was difficult since a distinguished geologist had already been invited to become Scientific Director, but eventually chose to withdraw rather than take a subordinate role. With Prime Minister Balfour's interest having finally secured Markham the official funding he sought, the Admiralty also agreed to provide another regular officer as second-in-command and two or three others from the Royal Naval Reserve. In fact they supplied rather more, let alone the bulk of the crew, most of whom were volunteers Scott had canvassed through friends in the Channel Squadron.

Notably, Scott chose a number of men from the *Majestic*: Lieutenants Michael Barne and Reginald Skelton (as chief engineer), Warrant Officer James Dellbridge as second engineer, and two petty officers, David Allan and Edgar Evans, who was the first to die returning from the Pole in 1912. The navigator and second-in-command was in the end a lieutenant Royal Naval Reserve (RNR): a P&O officer called Albert Armitage who had been part of the Jackson–Harmsworth Arctic Expedition to Franz Josef Land (1894–1897). The first lieutenant, 23-year-old Charles Royds, had recently been commanding a torpedo-boat destroyer. The last officer was a merchant navy second mate called Ernest Shackleton, making his polar debut as a specially rated sub-lieutenant RNR. He came on leave from the Union Castle Line, having first used his considerable charm on the son of Llewellyn Longstaff, the expedition's main private sponsor, and then on Scott himself to secure a place. He had excellent experience in sail and steam, an out-going personality and a natural leader's ability to get men working together. In the long term, however, these qualities would give rise to underlying tensions with Scott's reserved character and tendency to be irritable under stress.

The regular officers all had scientific functions – Royds being the meteorologist, for example – but there was also a

A group photograph of the officers and men of *Discovery*. Scott is in the centre and Shackleton is standing fifth from the left. Unknown photographer, 1901.

civilian scientific complement. Louis Bernacchi, a Tasmanian who had wintered at Cape Adare with Borchgrevink was the physicist, particularly concerned with the magnetic work, and joined the ship in New Zealand. Hartley Ferrar, a recent Cambridge graduate, and Thomas Vere Hodgson of the Plymouth Marine Biological Laboratory joined as geologist and biologist respectively. Dr Reginald Koettlitz (known as 'Cutlets' and at 40 the oldest member of the expedition) had been with Armitage in the Arctic and was senior surgeon and botanist. His assistant, both medically and as naturalist, was Dr Edward Adrian Wilson, the artistically gifted and deeply Christian peacemaker of both Scott's voyages, known ten years later as 'Uncle Bill'. Though initially closer to Shackleton, he was to become the confidant and companion on whom Scott, not himself religious and also prone to self-doubts, came most personally to rely: 'a brave, true man – the best of comrades and the staunchest of friends' as he wrote to Wilson's wife when both lay dying in their tent in 1912.

The question of what vessel would be used was faced by the Ship Committee long before Scott appeared. The committee was chaired by Admiral Sir Francis Leopold McClintock who, as a captain, had solved the Franklin riddle 40 years before. Markham had known him since those days and was much influenced by him (and was later his biographer). McClintock's method of man-hauling sledges – which employed the manpower available to him – had subsequently become a practical orthodoxy for Royal Naval Arctic expeditions and, less justifiably, one that time hallowed with 'manly' moral weight. In hindsight, this is difficult fully to understand given that McClintock was a good dog driver and that naval expeditions as far back as Parry's in the early 1820s had experience of dogs from Inuit practice, some copying it. Part of the answer lies in numerical ratios: dogs are most effective as 'primary traction' when few men are involved. Otherwise, the number of dogs required becomes impractical. In the matter of a ship, however, the experience of McClintock and his colleagues produced a winner.

Markham himself visited Norway in 1898, as did Scott, to consult the explorer Fridtjof Nansen about potential steamships and to look at the possibility of having a vessel built similar to the *Fram*, in which Nansen had made his own epic voyage towards the North Pole in 1893–1896. Later to be Amundsen's ship, the *Fram* was designed to be squeezed up out of heavy pack ice that might threaten to crush it. This came to nothing, though, as did the idea of using various wooden whalers including the old *Bloodhound*, which under the name HMS *Discovery* had been one of the ships taken to the Arctic in 1875–1876 by another Ship Committee member, Sir George Nares. The end result was that a new wooden steam-auxiliary sailing ship was designed, based on Nares's *Discovery*. Significant modifications were made, and principal among them was a massively strengthened 'ice-breaker' bow, a rounded overhanging stern to resist ice pressure, and a carefully calculated use of ferrous metals to make the vessel a suitable platform to conduct geomagnetic experiments. Designed by Sir William Smith and laid down by the Dundee Shipbuilders Company, who were well experienced in building polar whalers, the new auxiliary barque was both one of the last three-masted wooden ships to be built and the first specially for scientific use since the little *Paramore* in 1694 (which was constructed for a voyage under the astronomer Edmond Halley). She was 52.4 metres (172 feet) long, 10 metres (33 feet) in the beam and weighed 1,570 tons, with sides 66cm (26 inches) thick and a coal-fired 450 indicated horsepower (i.h.p.) triple-expansion engine. On 21 March 1901, with Markham, Scott and many others present, Lady Markham launched the ship at Dundee as the *Discovery* – a name first borne into Arctic polar ice by one of Cook's ships in the 1770s.

Discovery sailed from London on 31 July 1901, cheered by large crowds and provisioned to support 47 men for three years – much of her supplies being donated by commercial sponsors. Off Cowes, King Edward VII came aboard with Queen Alexandra and invested Scott with the Royal Victorian Order. On 3 October she stopped briefly to refit and replenish stores at Cape Town en route for Lyttelton, New Zealand, where she docked on 29 November. On the way, to begin the magnetic survey work, Scott diverted far south over the 60th parallel, encountered their first ice and called at the deserted Macquarie Island, where the crew reacted well to the addition of penguin to their diet. The ship proved a slow sailer and heavy on coal when steaming but was otherwise an excellent sea-boat in the worst conditions. At Lyttelton her rigging was reset and stores replenished, with the gift of 45 live sheep being added to the 23 sledge dogs carried on deck. Again cheered by crowds, she sailed on 21 December, though immediately put into Port Chalmers to bury a seaman called Charles Bonner who was killed falling from the masthead. He and a deserter were replaced by two volunteers from an accompanying warship, HMS *Ringarooma*. One was Able Seaman Thomas Crean, henceforth the most indestructible and permanent figure in both Scott and Shackleton's stories. The addition of Stoker William Lashly proved to be valuable, as he was to be one of the heroes of Scott's last expedition.

On 2 January 1902 *Discovery* saw her first icebergs and began to push through a 435km (270-mile) belt of pack ice,

Discovery was launched on 21 March 1901. She was the first purpose-built British polar exploration ship designed to resist ice pressure and allow geomagnetic experiments on board. Photograph by Watt, Dundee, 1901.

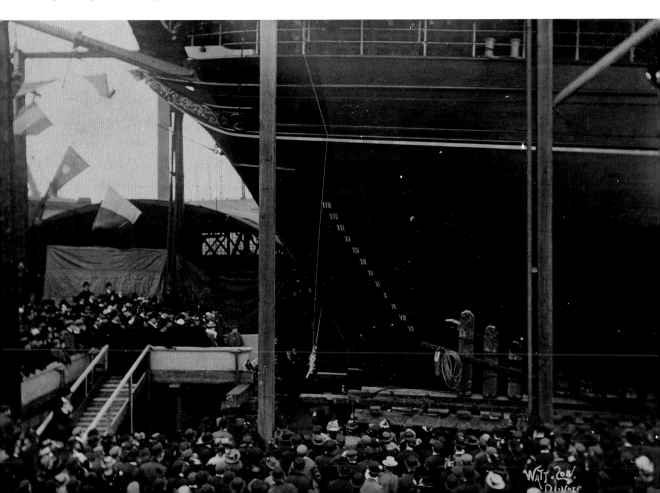

An informal photograph of Scott seeing King Edward VII and Queen Alexandra off after their visit to *Discovery* at Cowes, August 1901; who took it is unknown.

amid which the crew tried their skis and slaughtered the sheep, seals and penguin for the larder, now that the cold would preserve the results. Scott's squeamishness about such necessary butchery is well recorded: compared to Amundsen who routinely killed sledge dogs to feed the other dogs – and his men – it was a significant weakness. On 8 January they landed near Cape Adare, visiting Borchgrevink's hut, before sailing on to seek winter quarters further south. They found McMurdo Sound full of ice, and on 23 January, after establishing a mail-drop for their relief ship *Morning* at Cape Crozier on Ross Island (which they later first recognised as such), they sailed east along the edge of the Ice Barrier itself. This had now receded since Ross first found it but was generally from 15 to 75 metres (50 to 240 feet) high above the sea. On 26 January *Discovery* reached

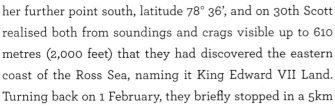

While the intention had been to live in the hut, Scott decided to use *Discovery* as accommodation. However, later expeditions used the hut as a refuge. LEFT

Shackleton's photograph of *Discovery*'s hydrogen balloon, *Eva*, being inflated on 3 February 1902. Scott and then Shackleton did the first balloon ascents in the Antarctic, the latter reaching a height of around 230 metres (750 feet). ABOVE

her further point south, latitude 78° 36', and on 30th Scott realised both from soundings and crags visible up to 610 metres (2,000 feet) that they had discovered the eastern coast of the Ross Sea, naming it King Edward VII Land. Turning back on 1 February, they briefly stopped in a 5km (3-mile) inlet in the ice front and from here a sledging party reached latitude 79° 03.5' (later revised to 78° 34') to examine the surface. Here Scott and Shackleton created another first, going up by balloon to survey the limitless plain. They saw no land in any direction, and Scott, who ascended first, nearly vanished for good by dropping too much ballast. Fortunately, the balloon was securely tethered but it developed a leak and was never used again.

Discovery returned to McMurdo Sound, which had cleared sufficiently to anchor in a sheltered inlet at what became known as Hut Point near the south end of Ross Island. By the end of March the ship was safely frozen in with huts erected ashore for auxiliary accommodation (though everyone in fact lived in the ship) and as observatories. By then George Vince, a seaman, had been killed while

The front cover of the first edition of the *South Polar Times*. This series continued an Arctic tradition of creating newspapers to inform and entertain the officers and crew.

on an abortive mission led by Royds to leave messages for *Morning* at Cape Crozier. He, Evans and others had been sent back in deteriorating weather when they slipped on a steep slope. Vince disappeared into the icy sea. Clarence Hare, the steward, was also presumed dead until he walked in over 36 hours later, having survived that time in the open. Experience was proving the best of teachers, but the costs were heavy. Before the winter night finally descended, everyone began to learn to ski and tried to get the dogs to work as sledge teams. In both cases the British were novices, to a degree now almost unimaginable, in skills that were almost native (certainly the skiing) to their Scandinavian compeers. Scott found skiing 'a pleasurable and delightful exercise' but was not convinced at first that it would be useful when dragging sledges. Despite liking his dogs, he was also not at ease with their savagery and the ruthlessness needed to manage them. For both Scott and Shackleton the cultural prejudice in favour of man-hauling sledges or using hardy ponies rather than dogs, against the urging of their Norwegian colleagues, was to prove near-fatal in their first voyages and, with other factors, finally so for Scott in 1911–1912.

Aside from regular scientific observations and the normal business of living, winter was taken up with activities that had been naval traditions in the Arctic. Amateur theatricals in the 'Royal Terror Theatre' (the hut) were high points, while Shackleton as editor and Wilson as illustrator put out five eagerly awaited typed editions of the *South Polar Times*. Time was also spent on preparing sledges and making up clothing and rations for the spring, and Scott did a great deal of relevant reading and laid plans for travelling south when light returned.

Scott's first sortie with two companions was a disaster. Two days later they struggled back with frostbite after their tent blew away in temperatures of -50°C. The next try saw him, Shackleton and Thomas Feather lay a large depot 137km

'THE PARSENGER'.

Shackleton was editor of the *South Polar Times* until he left in 1903. Dr Wilson created most of the illustrations that accompanied the poems, stories and articles, as seen on this page.

(85 miles) south of the ship. Feather fell down a crevasse, from which Scott rescued him, but with difficulty. On their return they found that scurvy had made its appearance among another party that had explored to the westward, living primarily on pemmican – a high-energy mixture of dried beef and lard that was a staple of all British polar expeditions. Scurvy was not then understood as a dietary deficiency, though fresh meat was known to prevent it, which led to a further round of seal hunting. On 2 November 1901, Scott, Shackleton and Wilson – with 19 dogs, five sledges, and skis – struck out on a major journey southwards, the Pole being the unstated objective. A second party of 12 under Barne manhauled in parallel with them to lay further depots until 15 November.

It was to prove a painful journey. The energy of the dogs soon waned, and there has since been debate about whether they had enough fresh meat in their winter feed, while the stockfish carried for them on Nansen's advice was both

Scott, Shackleton and Wilson, with the Depot Party, leaving for the attempt on the South Pole. Unknown photographer, 2 November 1902.

Wilson and Scott at the camp set up at their furthest south on 30–31 December 1902. They had mapped 483km (300 miles) of new coastline. Photograph by Shackleton. LEFT

'Long beards, hair dirty, swollen lips & peeled complexions, & blood-shot eyes [that] made them almost unrecognisable' was how Scott, Wilson and Shackleton were described on returning to *Discovery*. Unknown photographer, 3 February 1903. BELOW

inadequate and partly contaminated due to previous poor storage. They soon began to die, forcing Wilson to feed the dead to the living and begin killing the weaker ones for the same purpose. Wilson rapidly became agonisingly snow-blind from his unwise habit of sketching, and Shackleton developed an ominous cough, eventually spitting blood. Scott's impatience also began to grate on the others as they crossed the featureless Barrier, with Wilson finding himself a moderating influence. Scott had also miscalculated the amount of pemmican they needed, and soon both hunger and scurvy began to bite. On 30 December, after celebrating Christmas with a miniature plum pudding brought by Shackleton, they had to turn back at 82°17' south, still 660km (410 miles) from the Pole. Having killed the last dogs, by then they were hauling their remaining sledges until, about 240km (150 miles) from home, Shackleton became incapable of doing more than stagger along on his own, occasionally sitting on the last sledge to act as a brake. In this desperate state, on 3 February they met Skelton and Bernacchi, who had come south to find them. In all they had travelled about 1,368km (850 miles), had been away for 93 days and had completed the longest sledging journey yet in Antarctica, as well as far exceeding the record for furthest south. They were all suffering from scurvy, exhaustion and malnutrition, and Shackleton's rapid decline had raised serious questions about his basic constitution and fitness.

On return to base they found that the *Morning* had arrived with orders for *Discovery* to sail for Lyttelton. However, she could not be broken from the ice and, rather than persist, Scott decided to spend another southern winter at Hut Point. When *Morning* sailed on 2 March she took eight men with her and Shackleton, whom Scott ordered home on medical grounds. However, this was much against Shackleton's wishes and was perhaps prompted by personality tensions that had begun to emerge on their southern journey.

During Scott's absence, Armitage had discovered a way up through the coastal mountains to the ice sheet of Victoria Land and the following October, 1903, Scott led a party up on to it. Again, blizzards reduced temperatures to -50°C and broken sledges caused a false start. When they set out again, they lost a vital navigational handbook in bad weather and took a risk in continuing beyond the safe limit of their supplies, eventually up to a height of 2,700 metres (8,900 feet). In mid-December, with the party now divided into two, Scott, Lashly and Evans refound the Ferrar Glacier (which they had ascended to reach the plateau) by the expedient of falling 90 metres (300 feet) down one of its upper slopes. Fortunately no one was hurt and Scott and Evans had an even more miraculous escape when they fell into a deep crevasse lower down, from which Lashly helped both to escape. They returned to *Discovery* on 24 December after 81 days and 1,767km (1,098 miles) of successful sledging – significantly, without dogs – to find that various other parties had also done well in other directions: Wilson to Cape Crozier investigating Emperor penguins; Royds and Bernacchi east over the Barrier; and Armitage surveying the Koettlitz Glacier. Lieutenant George Mulock, who had replaced Shackleton from the *Morning*, had surveyed more than 200 mountains, consolidating the picture of the 480km (300 miles) of coastline that the expedition as a whole added to the map.

Scott's worry was now whether *Discovery* would be freed from the ice to sail with *Morning*, when she again arrived from Lyttelton. There were about 32km (20 miles) of it between her and open water at the beginning of January 1904 when he and Wilson made a sortie northwards to investigate. What they found on 5 January was not only the *Morning* but also another ship, the larger *Terra Nova*, accompanying her, both sent by the Admiralty following much debate and anxiety at home about the expedition's safety. Scott now received firm orders that if the ice persisted, *Discovery* was to be abandoned. It proved to be touch-and-go, with the ship still beset by about 3km (2 miles) of ice in early February. Then on 14th, the combined effects of ocean swell and explosives allowed the relief vessels to reach her. Two days later *Discovery* was completely free, the last alarm being when a gale drove her pounding onto a shoal as they were manoeuvring out round Hut Point on 17th. For Scott, 'the hours that followed were truly the most dreadful I have ever spent', but the situation was saved by a shift of current and the ship sustained only relatively minor damage. All three ships headed north for New Zealand, with *Morning* under sail since Captain Colbeck (Borchgrevink's companion) had given up much of her coal to *Discovery*. They entered Lyttelton

Four men preparing explosive charges to blast a route through sea ice to free *Discovery*. Photograph possibly by JD Morrison, January–February 1904. LEFT

A triple explosion of guncotton in the pack ice to break it up. After a period of about six weeks the *Discovery* was finally freed. Photograph possibly by JD Morrison, January–February 1904. BELOW

Scott on skis returning from *Morning*, one of two relief ships sent to free *Discovery* or abandon her and take off the expedition crew. Photograph by William Colbeck, January–February 1904. LEFT

together to a rapturous welcome on Good Friday, 1 April 1904. The expedition had made the first long-distance penetration of the Antarctic continent and the scientific results – geographical, geological and biological, as well as in areas such as magnetic surveying and meteorology – were substantial. They filled many volumes, and the existence today of the Scott Polar Research Institute at Cambridge is, in part, a longer-term legacy of the work done under him on the *Discovery* voyage.

Nimrod, 1907–1909

On Shackleton's return to England in June 1903, he was quickly drawn into the row caused by Scott's decision to spend two winters in Antarctica. This had not been the approved original intention unless unavoidable, and some saw the failure to free *Discovery* from the ice as incompetence or conspiracy. It became a public issue when, with expedition funds exhausted, the Admiralty felt obliged to underwrite a relief voyage, not only for *Morning* but to buy and send the *Terra Nova* as well. Under Markham's guidance, Shackleton publicly defended the expedition and helped fit out *Terra Nova*, but he declined to sail with her.

The only comment he made to me about not reaching the Pole, was 'a live donkey is better than a dead lion, isn't it?'

Emily Shackleton, 1922

Shackleton had been born in County Kildare, Ireland, on 15 February 1874, to a landed Anglo-Irish Protestant family. From 1880 they lived in Dublin and in 1884 his father, now a doctor, moved them to Sydenham, south London. Ernest was the second child and, like Scott, the elder of two brothers, though with eight rather than four sisters. Like Scott, he was educated at home until he was 11 and went on to Dulwich College, the local middle-class public school. He was not academic but loved reading and poetry, especially Browning's, which he was later wont to quote endlessly. He was well-liked, addicted to tales of adventurous romance, often in mild trouble and famously inventive in talking himself out of it. By 16 he had decided he wanted to go to sea and in an attempt to rid him of this desire, his father's cousin found him a berth as ship's boy on a square-rigger

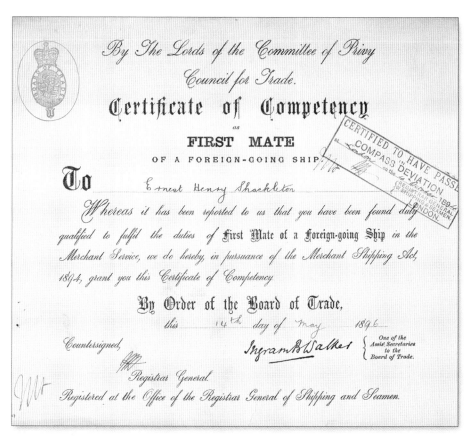

By The Lords of the Committee of Privy Council for Trade.

Certificate of Competency

as

FIRST MATE

OF A FOREIGN-GOING SHIP

To

Ernest Henry Shackleton

Whereas it has been reported to us that you have been found duly qualified to fulfil the duties of **First Mate** of a **Foreign-going Ship** in the Merchant Service, we do hereby, in pursuance of the Merchant Shipping Act, 1894, grant you this Certificate of Competency

By Order of the Board of Trade,

this 14th day of May 1896

Countersigned,

Ingram B Walker

{ One of the Assist. Secretaries to the Board of Trade.

Registrar General.

Registered at the Office of the Registrar General of Shipping and Seamen.

CERTIFIED TO HAVE PASSED in COMPASS DEVIATION

Shackleton's first mate's certificate, 1896. He had a varied early career in sailing and steam merchant shipping before signing up for the 1901 British Antarctic expedition.

outward bound for Valparaiso round Cape Horn. It confirmed rather than cured his seafaring streak: he signed on, spent the next four years in the same ship and gained a second mate's certificate. He then transferred to steam tramping, mainly to the Far East, and in April 1898, aged 24, obtained a master's certificate. The following year he joined the Union Castle Line on the South Africa run, also becoming a Fellow of the Royal Geographical Society (RGS) as a matter of personal interest in exploration.

Shackleton was third mate of the *Tintagel Castle* when he met Cedric Longstaff, son of the *Discovery* expedition's main private sponsor, going out on the ship with his regiment to the Boer War in 1900. By this time he had also fallen in love with Emily Dorman, a friend of one of his sisters, whose prosperous solicitor father liked him but did not approve of him as a match. A combination of restlessness, the appeal of patriotic adventure and the wish to distinguish himself and win Emily led him to volunteer for Scott's expedition, obtaining an introduction from young Longstaff to his father – also a keen Fellow of the RGS.

Scott's decision to order Shackleton home in 1902 was an affront both to his aspirations and his professional self-esteem. It called his fitness into question and implied he had not been frank about it when joining the expedition. This was a sensitive point, for Shackleton avoided medical examinations if possible. Though physically and mentally tough, he seems to have had or developed an inkling that his constitution was suspect, but refused to acknowledge it. After the southern journey, Koettlitz formally examined him at Scott's request and inconclusively suggested asthmatic tendencies. Only after his death in 1922, aged 47, was it discovered that he also had long-standing coronary heart disease. When this began is unknown but neither his smoking nor the privations he willingly endured would have helped either of these conditions.

By 1902 Shackleton had also witnessed Scott's qualities as a leader. Scott was a conventional, class-conscious naval officer whose social charm masked ambitiously devious traits. His authority was based on position rather than personality and, even allowing for his polar inexperience, he had made a number of serious mistakes. By contrast, Shackleton had an easy, charismatic rapport with most of the expedition – both officers and men, as in his other ships – and a more innate confidence in his own leadership abilities. He had no doubt that Scott felt his leadership had been challenged and that Shackleton's temporary breakdown was a useful pretext on which to banish him. This was confirmed when Scott returned home. In a major lecture and the published account of the *Discovery* expedition, he subtly blamed Shackleton's health for their failure to get further south in 1902, minimised his own and Wilson's debilities, and overstated how they had had to pull Shackleton to safety as a passenger on the sledge. This was humiliating to Shackleton, though he did not show it in his relations with Scott. He had not, of course, dwelt on his own problems and now had a reputation – in

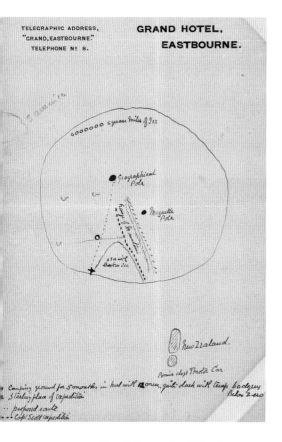

A 1907 hand-drawn sketch by Shackleton outlining his original proposed route to the South Pole from the opposite side of the Ross Sea to where Scott intended to operate.

fact several – to maintain. In the interim he had become Secretary of the Royal Scottish Geographical Society, was briefly a parliamentary candidate and a journalist, and was involved in various other uncertain business ventures in which his self-presentation was his main asset. He had also at last married Emily, to win whom he had, in part, originally joined *Discovery*.

Almost as soon as he returned, Shackleton unsuccessfully urged Markham to help him mount his own expedition to reach either Pole as a deliberate aim rather than under scientific cover. This would be his vindication. He and Scott remained civil in public but were henceforth to avoid each other. However, Scott's undermining (as Shackleton saw it) was not his sole spur: others included the dramatic Argentine rescue of Larsen and Otto Nordenskjöld from the Weddell Sea in 1903 after their ship *Antarctic* was crushed by ice; the Scottish explorer WS Bruce's return to the Clyde (and a welcome that Shackleton organised) from a successful private expedition in the same area; and Amundsen's first traverse of the North-West Passage in 1903–1906. In the background, too, were ongoing American plans to reach the North Pole.

By February 1907 Shackleton had his wish and launched an entirely private Antarctic expedition on a sea of large commercial hopes and rather less ready money. A loan of £1,000 from an eccentric lady admirer, a £7,000 guarantee from the Scottish industrialist William Beardmore – for whom Shackleton briefly worked and whose wife was a close confidante – and the promise of backing by a mining speculator who would obtain mineral rights to any such resources found, were the three main elements. Further returns were to come from the articles, lecturing, books and even the film that Shackleton saw himself producing on his return.

The 'British Antarctic Expedition 1907' was organised with astonishing speed, not least because Shackleton unsuccessfully asked both Wilson and Mulock to join him and found out from the latter that Scott was already thinking of a second expedition. Shackleton realised that he would stand to lose in a public confrontation with Scott and he sought to avoid one. In this his main disappointment was to find Wilson's moral weight firmly behind Scott's demand that he abandon his plan to use the McMurdo Sound base, to which Scott claimed exclusive rights. His greatest mistake, when Scott grandly extended his proprietary claims to the entire Victoria Land side of the Ross Sea, was to sign a written promise to base himself on the eastern side and under no circumstance stray west of the 170th meridian.

Shackleton's preparations were similar to Scott's yet also unlike them. Rather than scientists and regular naval men, he recruited adventurers. Some, like himself, were of respectable background, but most were restless and unconventional. He visited Norway to obtain equipment and consulted Nansen, now Norwegian minister in London, but then ignored his and other Norwegian advice to use skis and dogs. The only dogs he took were nine picked up at the last minute in New Zealand. Instead he was persuaded by Frederick Jackson to buy 12 Manchurian ponies, despite the fact that Jackson's own work with horses in Franz Josef Land had not been successful. This and his intention to walk rather than ski were more remarkable because his original idea was to march beyond the Pole dragging a light boat, with which he planned to rejoin his ship at a rendezvous in the Weddell Sea. The boat was accidentally left behind but even Shackleton had by then realised that crossing the continent was impractical. Beardmore, however, did give him a specially adapted car – the first to be used there. It did not live up to his hopes: while it worked to a useful degree on firm ground, it was hopeless on snow. He remained bedevilled by inadequate finances, not least when his minerals backer failed to deliver. A final bizarre threat to his public credit arose when his shady businessman brother and adviser, Frank, was implicated in a high-profile scandal surrounding the theft of the Irish coronation regalia. As for a ship, all he could afford was a 40-year-old, 300-ton auxiliary sealer called *Nimrod*, which

A postcard of the expedition ship *Nimrod*, with an inset portrait of Shackleton. Such items illustrate the public interest in Antarctic expeditions and their leaders.

sailed from London on 30 July 1907 under command of Rupert England, previously first mate of *Morning*.

Scott's well-funded expedition had been two years in the making, while Shackleton's hand-to-mouth one took barely seven months to prepare. By royal command, *Nimrod* stopped in the Solent during Cowes week under the guns of the Home Fleet drawn up in massive review. Edward VII and Queen Alexandra came aboard and Shackleton, like Scott, was awarded the Royal Victorian Order and presented with a Union flag by the Queen. *Nimrod* then sailed for New Zealand. Shackleton followed by steamer from Marseilles via Suez to Australia, after a last desperate round of fundraising and a guilty farewell to the understanding Emily, who was left to manage on her own modest private means with two small children.

In Australia, Shackleton was an immediate public hit, gaining much-needed support. Scientific credibility was boosted by his recruitment of an eminent Welsh-born geologist, Professor Edgeworth David, whose influence secured him a £5,000 grant from the Australian government. With him came an old pupil, Douglas Mawson, whom Shackleton nominated as expedition physicist. Both had only originally asked to sail out and back on *Nimrod*, and David's intention to remain throughout was concealed until he was beyond reach. Both men went on to gain Antarctic fame and knighthoods, and Mawson found himself at the head of later expeditions. New Zealand supplied £1,000 and half the cost of towing *Nimrod* to the Antarctic, once it became clear she was already too overloaded to carry enough coal and had to leave five ponies and other stores behind. The tow, by the *Koonya* under Frederick Evans, was an epic of skill, storm and appalling discomfort, ending on 15 January 1908 just inside the Antarctic Circle.

Shackleton's resolve to base himself on the eastern side of the Ross Sea was immediately broken, to his own great regret and with later public recriminations of bad faith from Scott and his supporters. The Barrier ice front had totally changed since 1902. Barrier Inlet, where they had made the balloon ascent, had vanished, while pack ice and lack of coal prevented an extended search for a landing anywhere other than McMurdo Sound. Shackleton set up a base at Cape Royds, Ross Island, as *Nimrod* was unable to reach Scott's anchorage at Hut Point because of ice. He and England seriously disagreed over the latter's handling of *Nimrod* in the difficult landing conditions, and on his return to Lyttelton, England found that the sealed orders he was carrying from Shackleton dismissed him. When this news and that of the broken promise to Scott reached home, they combined with embarrassing revelations about both Frank Shackleton's affairs and Ernest's irregular use of expedition loans. Shackleton was now more than geographically isolated: debts were mounting, sponsors alienated and for a while even money for his relief by *Nimrod* was lacking.

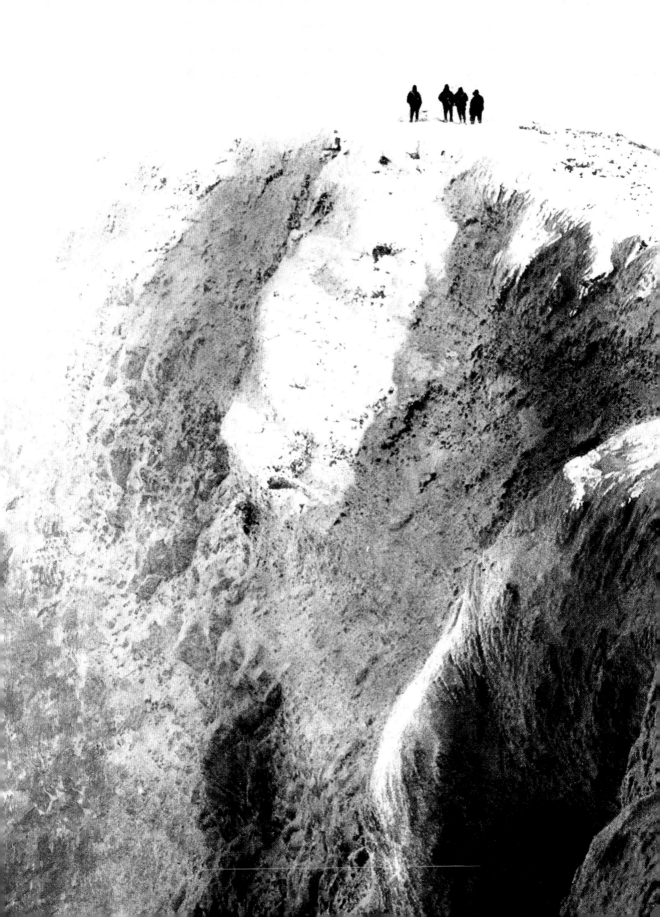

Before winter set in, the only achievement at Cape Royds was a hazardously impromptu first ascent of Mount Erebus in March 1908. Eric Marshall, the surgeon, forbade Shackleton to undertake it unless he passed fit. Shackleton declined to be examined and the climb was made by the 50-year-old David, Mawson, Lieutenant Adams (the expedition's second-in-command), the two doctors Marshall and Mackay, and Sir Philip Brocklehurst, the 20-year-old baronet adventurer of the party. This triumph of amateur mountaineering to the smoking crater, conducted without even proper boots and dogged by altitude sickness, fixed Erebus's height at 4,115 metres (13,500 feet).

Shackleton's style was very different from Scott's. There was no 'wardroom' or 'mess-deck' in his hut: everyone lived together, though Shackleton's one distinction as leader was having a personal sleeping cubicle. There were tensions but his outward confidence and the courteous maturity of David maintained a working equilibrium through the winter, helped by Marshall's quite advanced dietary regime, which included both plenty of fresh seal meat and tinned fruit and tomatoes (all anti-scorbutic in effect). As with Scott, no serious attempt was made to perfect the use of either skis or the dogs, who were growing bored from lack of exercise. When Shackleton began shuttling supplies to Hut Point over the sea ice in August, it was all by man-hauling and using the car for the few miles of hard surface over which it would run.

In early October, David, Mawson and Mackay left on an epic journey of their own up to the Victoria Land plateau to accomplish Ross's old dream of reaching the South Magnetic Pole. On 3 November, having laid an advanced depot 160km (100 miles) south of Hut Point, Shackleton, Adams, Marshall and Wild set off with their four surviving ponies and, until 7th, an initial support party, to reach the South Pole. Shackleton calculated this at 1,202km (747 miles) from Cape Royds, and he hoped the journey would be a straight and relatively level march over the Barrier. They had 91 days' food and allowing that it might be stretched to 110, this meant covering at least 20km (12.5 miles) a day. The dogs (inadequate in number) were left behind. The feet of ponies and men without skis sank into the snow at

Reaching the summit of Mount Erebus was their first success. 'We stood on the verge of a vast abyss [with] a huge mass of steam filling the crater.' Photograph by Douglas Mawson, 10 March 1908. OPPOSITE

every step but by 26 November they had passed the most southerly point of Scott and Shackleton's first journey in 29 days, compared to 59.

By 1 December they had only one pony left, the other three having been shot and depoted for food as they weakened. Ahead the Barrier ended in a line of mountains, which they could not have known were the 4,800m (3,000-mile) Transantarctic Range, peeling off inland from the Ross Sea. Two days later, crossing massive pressure ridges of ice, they climbed a low pass dubbed the Gateway and discovered beyond it their cause – the rising, awesome 160km (100-mile) sweep of what Shackleton was later to name the Beardmore Glacier, falling off the polar plateau. This was one of the few ways up through the mountains and had ample hazards of its own. These quickly became clear when their last pony vanished through the snow into one of the hundreds of hidden crevasses, itself a shocking enough event, but one that also deprived them of its meat. By Christmas Day they were some 2,895 metres

Shackleton, Wild and Adams at their furthest south (lat. 88° 23'). Shackleton recorded: 'Our last day outwards. We have shot our bolt... whatever regrets may be, we have done our best.' Photograph by ES Marshall, 9 January 1909.

(9,500 feet) up at the top, 885km (550 miles) from 'home' and with about 400km (250 miles) to go to the Pole. They had less than a month's supplies left, and their average speed was down to about 15km (9.5 miles) a day against the still rising and difficult ground, as well as continuous headwinds and blizzards, which on some days stopped them from leaving their tent.

By New Year's Day 1909 they were nonetheless closer than anyone had been before to either the North or South Poles, but altitude sickness was seriously affecting Shackleton in particular, as they crossed the 3,353-metre (11,000-foot) contour in temperatures around -30°C. This they endured with inadequate clothing, having discarded as much as possible to save weight, with the result that their body temperatures were technically below critical level. They were also increasingly malnourished. At 4am on 9 January 1909, as another blizzard died away, they left their tent and sledge to make a final dash south and plant the Union flag Queen Alexandra had given them at 88° 23' south. This was just 156km (97 miles) from the Pole, 589km (366 miles) beyond Scott's furthest south. Having taken photographs, they immediately turned back, now with the wind behind them and helped by a sail made from a tent floor-cloth. Already weak, their survival was entirely dependent on following their own outward tracks and finding the small depots they had left on the way – a task made more difficult when they lost the sledgemeter wheel, which counted off the miles as they went. On 20 January, with just one day's food left and starvation looming, they found their first depot and extra clothing near the head of the Beardmore Glacier. At this point, even though the altitude was now decreasing rapidly, Shackleton collapsed with breathing difficulty and a high temperature, and for some time had to be carried on the sledge. It was almost a repeat of the *Discovery* journey, though without critical scurvy. Fortunately the weather was good but by the time they were very close to the next depot 64km (40 miles) on, everyone was so exhausted that only Marshall was able to reach it and bring back food. Finally, down on the Barrier, Shackleton recovered but the same desperate sequence was repeated, depot by depot, with dysentery added to the mix when they ate meat from a pony left at the base of the glacier.

The southern party finally on board *Nimrod* (left to right: Wild, Shackleton, Marshall, Adams). Shackleton wrote: 'We had been given up for 10 days past & killed in a hundred different ways.' Unknown photographer, 4 March 1909. OPPOSITE

As the last 480km (300 miles) slowly wore them down, all that saved them was generally fair weather, willpower, and finally help from the party left at Cape Royds. This took the form of a large cairned depot 80km (50 miles) south of Hut Point, which, following orders left by Shackleton, Joyce and others had laid in two journeys beginning on 15 January. For this, Joyce had successfully used dogs, having taken the interest and effort to form them and himself into an adequate team, with impressive results. Shackleton reached this point and plentiful food on 23 February but knew he had only five days left to return to Hut Point before *Nimrod*, which Joyce's note confirmed had now arrived, would sail for New Zealand, giving his party up for dead. In fact this had already been assumed: they were now a month overdue in terms of the food supply with which they had started. Consequently, lookouts who should have been posted for them from 25 February were not on station.

In the end, with Marshall no longer able to continue, Shackleton and Wild made a 40-hour, 48km (30-mile) forced march, practically without food and only brief rest, to the *Discovery* hut, arriving on the evening of 28 February. It was unexpectedly deserted and unsupplied, with an ominous note from David saying everyone else was safe but implying that *Nimrod* might have already sailed. Despair loomed until the following morning, when the ship, now commanded by Evans from the *Koonya*, returned from a safer offing to land a small wintering party under Mawson. This had been hastily arranged after much argument on board, the sole purpose being to search for the bodies of the southern party. Shackleton – who had not slept properly for more than 50 hours – insisted on immediately leading the rescue of Marshall and Adams, a further two-day and nearly 100km (60-mile) march out and back on foot, since the dogs were waiting for collection at Cape Royds. It was an extraordinary demonstration of both responsibility and endurance, given his earlier collapse and exhausted state. When they returned on 3 March, he immediately ordered *Nimrod*'s departure for New Zealand, abandoning part of their baggage and equipment ashore rather than add a further day's risk of being trapped in the gathering ice of the southern winter.

**Despite the Royal Geographical Society's
reluctance** to recognise the *Nimrod*
voyage's achievements, they issued a gold
medal to Shackleton and silver replicas to
members of the expedition. LEFT

FURTHEST SOUTH

THE ADVENTUROUS VOYAGE OF THE "DISCOVERY," AND THE SLEDGE JOURNEY TO THE FURTHEST POINT SOUTH EVER REACHED BY MAN.

BY LIEUTENANT E. H. SHACKLETON, ONE OF THE THREE OFFICERS WHO REACHED THE MOST SOUTHERLY LATITUDE YET ATTAINED.

PART II.

OF THE SLEDGE-PARTIES already referred to, one, consisting of three officers, went out to examine the land to the South, to see if it were possible to proceed on any lengthened journey in that direction; another, under Lieutenant Royds, to try and place a record at Cape Crozier; and another, under the captain, to establish a depôt towards the South. These expeditions were hampered by the extreme cold and the unsuitable conditions of the weather at that time. It was during the return of a portion of Lieutenant Royds' party, under Lieutenant Barne, that the only fatal accident occurred. One of the

men, in a furious blizzard, fell over an ice cliff and was drowned. One must be on the spot to realise what these blizzards mean, when nothing can be seen while the wind lasts, and it is fortunate that more were not lost throughout the whole Expedition. In spite of the most careful management and attention to detail in the work of sledging, these accidents are liable to occur. All that man could do for the safety of his party was done on that occasion by Lieutenant Barne. He himself suffered most severely, being badly frostbitten. His resource and care have made him deservedly popular with the men who served under him.

PHOTOGRAPH BY LIEUTENANT SHACKLETON.

THE END OF THE ONLY BALLOON ASCENT IN THE ANTARCTIC, FEBRUARY 4, 1902: DEFLATING THE BALLOON.

The captive balloon ascent took place at an inlet in the Barrier, and was the first ever made from a field of ice or under such weather conditions as then prevailed. The balloon, which ascended 750 feet, was inflated with hydrogen carried by the "Discovery." Owing to the peculiar atmospheric conditions, it required 1000 cubic feet more gas than it would have done in a more temperate climate. Note in the rigging the ship's larder of seal-meat.

WHITE WARFARE **3**

by Diana Preston

'A period of badly strained optimism' was how HG Wells described the opening years of the 20th century. While predicting a world of aeroplanes, air-conditioning and cosy suburban living, he also foresaw wars more widespread than the conflict with the Boers, in which Britain was engaged as 1900 began. No one was yet quite sure who the enemy would be. Some newspapers warned that the French might launch a combined forces raid on London while Britain was distracted in South Africa. Later, as the Germans began to build a navy to rival Britain's dreadnoughts, they became the more likely enemy.

Much to the glee of Britain's rivals, the war in South Africa had not gone well initially. There were major defeats at Spion Kop and elsewhere. Robert Baden-Powell and his men were besieged in Mafeking and were only relieved with much difficulty. Nevertheless, the mad rejoicing in the streets at the relief brought a new word into the vocabulary, to 'maffick'. 'Mother may I go and maffick, rush around and hinder traffic?' went one rhyme, not without irony. But this could not mask fears that modern Britons were becoming decadent compared with their forebears. Baden-Powell – soon to found the Boy Scouts and already an instant hero for his role in the siege – saw disturbing parallels with the decadence and decline of the Roman Empire. He warned of the dangers of physical degeneracy. He recalled how the Romans had come to grief because their soldiers 'fell away from the standard of their forefathers in bodily strength'.

Such self-doubt and uncertainty fuelled a hunger for heroes as tangible reaffirmation of Britain's greatness. But these heroes must not be swaggering, bragging types. Britain's dignity had long demanded understated, self-deprecating heroes, unfailingly cheerful in the face of adversity. When Livingstone was

Captain R. F. SCOTT, R.N.

Died March 29th, 1912, at the South Pole.

" We bow to the will of providence determined
" still to do our best to the last. These rough
" notes and our dead bodies must tell the tale."
R. Scott.

'A British Hero'. A souvenir postcard
of Captain Scott and the *Terra Nova* in
an Antarctic landscape, published after
Scott's death. It shows how he was by then
presented to the British public.

buried in Westminster Abbey in 1874, the press lauded 'the brave, modest, self-sacrificing African explorer', enthusing that such virtues were those 'which our country has always been ready to acknowledge, which our religion has taught us to revere, and seek to cultivate and conserve'. Baden-Powell himself seemed to embody the stiff upper lip, sending laconic telegrams from Mafeking such as 'All well. Four hours bombardment. One dog killed.' So keen were the myth makers to reinforce this image that they even claimed Baden-Powell never cried during childhood.

Edwardians thought that men should behave heroically for King, country and comrades, not out of personal ambition. Also, while winning was important, it was not everything. The good sport and the plucky loser were held in huge esteem. Although Britain topped the medals table with 56 gold medals at the 1908 Olympic Games at London's White City, some of the loudest applause greeted Queen Alexandra's presentation of a consolation gold cup to the Italian marathon runner Durando Pietri. He had collapsed while leading in the final lap and been disqualified for receiving help over the finish line. In one of the rowing events at Henley, the British team chivalrously waited for their Dutch opponents to resume rowing after they had run their boat into the bank.

The ideal hero in a society steeped in the works of GA Henty, Rudyard Kipling and Conan Doyle also embodied a certain boyish, schoolboy fervour. JM Barrie, creator of Peter Pan and friend of Captain Scott, captured this somewhat naïve spirit in his introduction to 'Like English gentlemen', an allegorical tribute written after Scott's death: 'And so this hero of heroes said, I am going to find the South Pole. It will be a big adventure.'

Antarctic exploration indeed seemed a 'big adventure' to the Edwardians, satisfying a number of needs in this society in transition. First, national pride and precedence required that Britain should claim the South Pole. The British had long been pre-eminent in Antarctic discovery, from the days of Captain Cook to James Clark Ross and beyond. Yet, on a deeper, psychological level, Antarctica represented an ultimate testing ground, a kind of quest for the Holy Grail, where Britons could demonstrate that they retained the manly attributes of old. Sir Clements Markham, the driving force behind the 1901–1904 *Discovery* expedition, fostered such thoughts, designing sledge flags like medieval pennants for the participants.

Antarctica's almost mystical remoteness was another factor. Like Barrie's 'Neverland', this place of mists and legends could not be seen by ordinary mortals. When Scott, Shackleton and the rest set off in 1901, it was to disappear behind an icy screen into *terra incognita* – a white, featureless wasteland. There had been many recent developments in communications. Telegraphs enabled Queen Victoria in 1897 to broadcast her message to the Empire at the single press of a button in Buckingham Palace and for it to pass through to Tehran within two minutes on its way to the furthest corners of her dominions. However, all such innovations were intriguingly and entirely irrelevant in Antarctica. Once the explorers had sailed over the southern horizon, the world could know nothing of their struggles and achievements until they, or a relief ship, emerged with news the following season.

Public interest in Antarctica was initially quite low-key. However, the popular press like the *Daily Mail* – launched in 1896 priced at half a penny and with circulation by 1900 of a million copies a day – had an appetite for heroes and new-found lands, and played an influential role. When the *Discovery* expedition was announced, the papers emphasised the quest for the Pole, rather than the scientific aspects. *The Morning Post* rejoiced: 'Even in the last throes of an exhausting struggle [the Boer War], we can yet spare the energy and the men to add to the triumphs we have already won in the peaceful but heroic field of exploration.'

They brought their readers the subsequent, joyful news that Scott, Shackleton and Wilson had reached within 645km (400 miles) of the Pole. When Sir Clements Markham, who feared a repeat of the Franklin tragedy, expressed anxiety

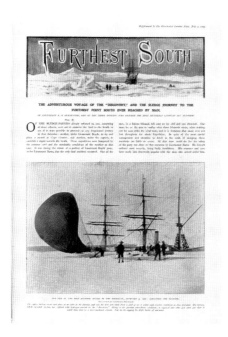

The special 'Furthest South' supplement in the *Illustrated London News* was written by Shackleton on his return in July 1903 and included some of his own photographs. ABOVE

A handbill advertising the first public lecture on the *Terra Nova* expedition, 4 June 1913. Illustrated lectures were an important way to engage audiences on a more personal level. Relatively high prices and professional organisation exploited their patriotic and human appeal. OPPOSITE

for the men's safety, the papers fuelled the public's anxiety. Would the men of the *Discovery* return safely? If so, would they be emaciated, exhausted skeletons, harrowed by unimaginable experiences? When the *Discovery* finally sailed into Portsmouth Harbour in September 1904, a surprised *Daily Express* journalist reassured his readers not only that the men looked like 'seasoned mahogany' but that, against all the odds, they had positively flourished.

The press alighted on Scott who discovered, somewhat to his dismay, that he had become a 'celebrity'. His remarks to journalists that the men of the *Discovery* had been very well able to take care of themselves, and had had no need of the relief vessel sent to find the party, endeared him to the public. Heroes were supposed to be self-sufficient, scornful of danger and disdainful of fuss. Scott was lionised by London society and invited to Balmoral by King Edward VII to report in person. He was made a CVO (Commander of the Royal Victorian Order), although he did not receive the rumoured knighthood. An *Antarctic Exhibition* staged by Markham at London's Bruton galleries, which included several hundred of Edward Wilson's inspirational drawings, a model of the *Discovery* and sledging equipment, drew 10,000 fascinated visitors. The fashionable world descended from their carriages, horseless or otherwise, to be told by the patient policemen that they would have to queue like everyone else. It was a new experience for them to have to wait their turn and perhaps a sign of the changing times. The exhibition's photographs of the *Discovery* trapped in the ice brought the scale, magic and danger of Antarctica home to people with a compelling immediacy. They were confronted by images of a world that until then had only existed in their imagination.

TOWN HALL, PORTSMOUTH.

Messrs. GODFREY & Co., Ltd., in co-operation with The Lecture Agency, Ltd., of London,
beg to announce that on

THURSDAY, OCTOBER 16th, at 8 p.m.,

COMMANDER EVANS

C.B., R.N.,

Will deliver a LECTURE on

"Capt. Scott's Expedition"

The Lecture will be fully
illustrated by Lantern Slides
and Kinematograph Films.

ADMIRAL THE HON.

SIR HEDWORTH MEUX,

G.C.B., K.C.V.O.,

WILL PRESIDE.

COMMANDER EVANS relates the wonderful
experiences of the various parties sent out
from the "Terra Nova," and tells how Captain
Scott and his brave companions, after reaching
the South Pole, struggled to the last against
overwhelming odds.

Capt. ROBERT FALCON SCOTT, C.V.O.

Numbered and Reserved Stalls, **7/6, 5/-, 3/-**; Front Row of Balcony (reserved), **5/-**;
Unreserved Seats, **2/-**; Admission, **1/-**

Plans & Tickets of Messrs. GODFREY & Co., Ltd., 74 Palmerston Rd., Southsea, & 91 Russell St., London.

PRO PATRIA

DURING the long ages that make up the history of our race and country, there
have been many episodes that can never die. One of these, and surely one of the
most glorious and inspiring, is that of Captain Robert Falcon Scott's march to the
South Pole and the heroic death of himself and his faithful comrades.

All the ventures of our countrymen into the frozen regions of the North and
South have been ennobled by the chivalry, the devotion to duty, that we love to think
inseparable from the British name; but none has more wonderfully filled us with
legitimate pride in the breed of men to which we belong than the story of the dauntless
Five—who, in the face of doom, wrought so much and so valorously for Britain.

The bodies of these brave men have fitting sepulture far from their island home;
but what they did, and how manfully they did it, must be very near and very dear to the
hearts of their countrymen, and shall endure for evermore.

There are words that come into the minds of the men of our blood and speech,
at that moment when the danger is greatest and odds are extreme, such as Mr. Henry
Newbolt has given us in "Play up! and play the game!" In the years ahead many
a Briton may find himself brought hand to hand with fate, and in the last dread
hour that tries the man the deathless message penned by the dying explorer will
brace the nerves and steel the courage. "Things have come out against us, and
therefore we have no cause for complaint, but bow to the will of Providence,
determined still to do our best to the last." Captain Scott and the men who fear-
lessly went with him into the Great Unknown accomplished much in their lives, but
it is the manner in which they gave up those lives that will make their names
immortal. All that they had that men desire they cheerfully placed on the desperate
hazard; they vanquished, and they knew defeat. But never was death more swallowed
up in victory. They died, and their glory—our heritage—is eternal. We are grateful,
and do homage to their memory.

"These rough notes and our dead bodies must tell the tale" are sacred words.
Those who knew Captain Scott can say how much they were in keeping with his
strong character, with the reticent and disciplined spirit that never failed—

"To set the cause above renown,
To love the game beyond the prize."

The leader of this gallant band was a hero through and through, and those who
perished with him were worthy of his leadership and of their everlasting fame.

Capt. L. E. G. OATES.

Dr. E. A. WILSON.

Capt.
R. F. SCOTT,
C.V.O., R.N.

Lieut. H. R. BOWERS, R.I.M.

Petty Officer EDGAR EVANS, R.N.

Part of the
ANTARCTIC REGIONS
Showing the Sphere of Operations
of the
BRITISH ANTARCTIC EXPEDITION, 1910-13
under
CAPT. R. F. SCOTT, R.N.

The full account of the British Antarctic Expedition, 1910-1912, based upon and supplementing
Captain Scott's Diary, will be issued in book form by Messrs. SMITH, ELDER & Co. in October

The whole of the arrangements for COMMANDER EVANS's lectures are under the Management
of Mr. GERALD CHRISTY, of THE LECTURE AGENCY, LTD., THE OUTER TEMPLE, STRAND,
LONDON, W.C.

Telephone GERRARD 200.   Telegram: "LECTURING, ESTRAND, LONDON."

Scott's lyrical account, *The Voyage of the 'Discovery'*, immediately sold out. The sentiments he expressed seemed a perfect rebuttal of all those fears about British decadence and decline. He scorned the use of dogs, asserting that the only truly 'manly' way was to pull the sledge yourself. He wrote: 'No journey ever made with dogs can approach the height of that fine conception … when men go forth … with their own unaided efforts and … succeed in solving some problems of the great unknown.' His philosophy was perfectly attuned to the ethos of his age. It is embodied in most Antarctic expeditions today.

What the public could not know was the personal impact the experience had had on their new hero. Scott was a fine writer and his book captured the siren beauty of Antarctica; but he could not reveal his personal feelings, the self-doubt and anxiety that had, on occasions, tormented him. A man of his time, he would have found it unthinkable to confess publicly to his lack of confidence and bouts of introspection, and it was certainly not what the public wanted from its hero. Yet, as he later confided in his wife, Kathleen, Antarctica had been a personal proving ground where he had battled as much against personal weaknesses as against the bitter physical conditions.

At the same time, like Shackleton, he had fallen in love with Antarctica. They had both been initially attracted to exploration through that unheroic thing – personal ambition. Neither were well-off and both had their way to make in the world. Scott was supporting his mother and sisters, while Shackleton wanted to establish himself in the eyes of his fiancée's wealthy family. But, as they sledged together across the Great Ice Barrier, ambition had fused with something else. Both had been gripped by Antarctica's astonishing beauty. Both had seen the possibilities it offered. Both felt compelled to return by what Shackleton termed the 'Call of the South', a kind of magnetic attraction.

Both also derived some wrong messages from their experiences. If either had been less insularly British, they would have realised from Norwegian experience that the failures of their dogs resulted partly from their own failures as dog-handlers. Had things been different, they would have relied mainly on dogs in their further expeditions and Shackleton would probably have been first to the

Pole in 1909. Scott and Shackleton's strong and very different personalities and the competitive tensions between them also fuelled a strong personal rivalry.

But, of course, this rivalry could not be aired in public. The attainment of the South Pole must be first and foremost for Britain's glory. When, in 1907, Shackleton announced his *Nimrod* expedition, Scott was angry at what he saw as trespassing on his territory, but his terse correspondence with Shackleton remained strictly private. All the public knew was that yet another British venture was underway. Shackleton's subsequent return in 1909, after sledging to within 156km (97 miles) of the Pole, was greeted with rapture and, within a few months, a knighthood. Shackleton was more comfortable with fame than Scott and relished courting the public. In articles about 'How I made for the South Pole', he charmed his readers with light-hearted tales of how the extreme cold had fuelled his passion for sweet puddings and how the explorers painted their hut with scenes of blazing fires and of Joan of Arc being burned to a crisp to 'convey at least an imagination of warmth'.

A master of public relations, Shackleton underplayed the drama of his experiences and this was approvingly noted. One paper proclaimed that: 'It is well that popular triumph should be accorded to other than military heroes. Lieutenant Shackleton and his companions have been the lions of the month, and never did a lion roar more modestly and more becomingly than the gallant hero, who in his speeches has shown a fund of dry humour not usually found among such men.'

Another rejoiced: 'We seem to be living in times when men have reverted to the age of the elemental heroes.'

Shackleton's decision to turn back, when so close to the Pole, was seen, in itself, as courageous. *The Dublin Express* comment that 'it is a brave thing to turn back'.

Lacking Scott's literary application, Shackleton employed a ghost writer to help him produce *The Heart of the Antarctic*, which was published to critical acclaim. One journal exulted: 'What may be done with a free hand by a man full of ability and confidence has been demonstrated this year by EH Shackleton.' It went on: 'He was fitted for his task by the possession

> *We seem to be living in times when men have reverted to the age of the elemental heroes.*

THE HEART OF
THE ANTARCTIC

The first edition of *The Heart of the Antarctic*. Both Scott and Shackleton recognised the importance of publishing their expedition experiences for a wider audience.

of great organising power, a vivid imagination, the originality of genius in devising plans, and sufficient experience on which to base them, but not enough to make caution hamper his ambition.' In other words, a hero's flair and daring mattered more than experience. It was a paean in praise of that most British phenomenon, the gifted amateur.

And it was as a gifted amateur that Scott again went south on the final, fatal *Terra Nova* expedition of 1910. Dogs were taken but not taken seriously. Many of Scott's colleagues were expert scientists but not one was an expert explorer. Two of the four men he was to take to the South Pole – Captain 'Titus' Oates and 'Birdie' Bowers – had never set foot on Antarctica before but had applied to join the expedition because it promised adventure. The other two, Edward Wilson and Edgar Evans, had been with Scott on the *Discovery* and had no more experience than their leader, to whom they felt great loyalty.

Scott's team contrasted starkly with Amundsen and his men. The Norwegian had chosen exploration as a career, cutting his teeth on Adrien de Gerlache's *Belgica* expedition, and was a focused 'professional' experienced in travel over snow and ice in the Arctic, and an expert skier and handler of dogs. From the moment Scott received the telegram from Amundsen informing him that he, too, was going south, Scott knew inwardly that the Norwegian might well beat him. This took a psychological toll. Yet publicly he had to preserve the good sportsmanship and coolness the public expected. Media 'hype' had prepared it for a British victory despite Amundsen's late intervention. Questioned by a journalist about his chances, Scott made the nonchalant response: 'We may get through, we may not. We may have accidents to some of our transports, to the sledges or to the animals. We may lose our lives. We may be wiped out. It is all a question that lies with providence and luck.' On the surface Scott had to appear cheerful and, above all, sporting. This was, after all, the era of good sports, the luck of the game and plucky losers.

We may lose our lives. We may be wiped out. It is all a question that lies with providence and luck.

And Scott was soon to be cast as the archetypal 'plucky loser'. The news that he had reached the Pole only to find himself beaten by Amundsen, and to perish on the return, prompted an immense national outpouring of grief on a scale comparable to the reaction to the death of Diana, Princess of Wales, in 1997. Headlines like 'Eight days starvation', 'His dying Appeal to England' and 'Homage to Heroes' held the country in thrall.

Scott with Kathleen on Quail Island, New Zealand, during a visit to the expedition ponies, November 1910. Her support and encouragement was vital for Scott, as she understood his insecurities.

The poignant photographs of the exhausted, downcast party at the Pole gave their tragedy a terrible immediacy. But it was above all Scott's letters and diaries, written in pencil because ink would have frozen, and found beneath his body, that fuelled the grief and sense of loss. If their

bodies, books, letters and photographic film had not been found, the impact would have been much less. They gave substance to the heroic image. People could relive, day by day, through his eyes, a truly epic tale of men battling bravely against ever-increasing odds; selflessly caring for their starving, frostbitten comrades; dragging their geological specimens with them until the end out of duty and pride but eventually succumbing in that blizzard-whipped green tent, just a few miles from a depot of supplies that might have saved them. He wrote of colleagues who were 'unendingly cheerful' although they knew they were doomed. Scott's understated, carefully chosen words resonated and formed an elegiac and heroic epitaph: 'Had we lived, I should have had a tale to tell ... which would have stirred the heart of every Englishman.'

Of course, his tale did stir hearts. In particular his account of Oates's death caused a collective lump in the throat and huge national pride. Here was a man who, rather than put his friends at risk, walked out into a blizzard to die with the briefest of comments: 'I am just going outside and may be some time.' It was the quintessential ideal of a British officer and gentleman – unsentimental, without self-pity, self-sacrificing. The *Daily Mail* lauded the 'immortal chivalry of Captain Oates'. His former army comrades were quick to write articles recalling his gritty valour during the Boer War, which had won him the nickname 'No Surrender Oates'. Ironically, the reopening of his old Boer War wound, one of the effects of scurvy, was probably a major contributor to his death.

Oates's real thoughts and feelings can only be guessed. During the dark Antarctic winter at Cape Evans he had told his comrades that anyone whose weakness was jeopardising other members of the team had a duty to shoot himself. His last letters betray a passionate attachment to life and longing for home, yet tortured by frostbite and denied his wish to die in his sleep, he had indeed contemplated suicide. His thoughts and feelings on the day he walked to his death were more complex than the public perception of simplistic heroes. Each reader must decide how much irony to read into those famous farewell words.

Similarly, the image of Scott that crystallised in the popular imagination was simplistic. His earlier letters to his wife, Kathleen, reveal his real self. It was only

THE DAILY MIRROR, Wednesday, May 21, 1913.

CAPTAIN SCOTT'S TOMB NEAR THE SOUTH POLE.

The Daily Mirror

24 Pages

THE MORNING JOURNAL WITH THE SECOND LARGEST NET SALE.

No. 2,987.   Registered at the G.P.O. as a Newspaper.   WEDNESDAY, MAY 21, 1913   One Halfpenny.

 THE MOST WONDERFUL MONUMENT IN THE WORLD: CAPTAIN SCOTT'S SEPULCHRE ERECTED AMID ANTARCTIC WASTES.

 It was within a mere eleven miles of One Ton camp, which would have meant safety to the Antarctic explorers, that the search party found the tent containing the bodies of Captain Scott, Dr. E. A. Wilson and Lieutenant H. R. Bowers. This is, perhaps, the most tragic note of the whole Antarctic disaster. Above is the cairn, surmounted with a cross, erected over the tent where the bodies were found. At the side are Captain Scott's skis planted upright in a small pile of frozen snow.—(Copyright in England. Droits de reproduction en France reservées.)

74

to her that he had felt safe to confide his dislike of the Navy and the rigidity that his creative, dreaming side had found so stifling: 'Knock a few shackles off me, you find as great a vagabond as you... I shall never fit in my round hole. The part of a machine has got to fit – yet how I hate it sometimes... I love the open air, the trees, the fields and the seas, the open spaces of life and thought.'

But private doubts had no place in a heroic tale. Just as Scott had concealed his true feelings in life, so they were suppressed after his death. Kathleen learned of her husband's death while she sailed south to New Zealand for what should have been their reunion. In deep despair she opened her diary and confided her feelings. She tried to comfort herself with the hope that, before he died, 'the horror of his responsibility left him, for I think never was there a man with such a sense of responsibility and duty...' The word 'horror' was replaced by 'weight' in the published version of the diary. The idea that Scott might have felt 'horror' at his responsibilities would have jarred with his heroic image. Just as with the human failings of Livingstone, General Gordon and Baden-Powell, his insecurities must not be revealed.

The press played a key role in Scott's metamorphosis into a national icon. They were quick to make comparisons with another recent and shocking tragedy, the sinking of the *Titanic* in April 1912, when women and children were flung into boats by men who knew themselves doomed, while the band played till the end. Papers reminded their readers that many of the British passengers had displayed the same cool courage and selfless concern for others. Even if there was increasing and uneasy acceptance of Darwin's theory that man was descended from the apes, and of Freud's emerging theories of the human psyche, Scott and his men, like the *Titanic*'s passengers, seemed to epitomise man's nobler instincts. But as one leader put it: 'Captain Scott died in more awful circumstances than the *Titanic*.'

The public were mesmerised. Thousands attended a memorial service in St Paul's. On the same day the 750,000 children of London's County Council schools were told Scott's story by their teachers. The *Daily Mirror* commented:

The *Daily Mirror* made showing the cairn built over Scott and his companions in November 1912 front page news, reflecting overwhelming public interest in the fate of the expedition. OPPOSITE

'What English boy or girl may not gain courage by saying "I will be brave as Captain Scott was – as he would wish me to be."' A memorial fund was flooded with far more money than Scott had managed, with much effort, to raise in sponsorship. Kathleen was given the status of a wife of a Knight Commander of the Order of the Bath, on the grounds that this honour would have been bestowed on Scott had he survived. She was a talented sculptress and was commissioned to create several statues of her husband.

Tales about heroes generally require villains. Amundsen, genuinely distressed by Scott's death and needlessly tormented by the thought that he should have left supplies for him at the Pole, was tailor-made for the role. He was foreign. He was seen as an interloper. Even worse, perhaps, he was a 'professional' whose tactics did not conform to the heroic 'amateur' mould. His achievements based on dogs rather than man-hauling seemed less virile and manly than Scott's. Put crudely, according to the chauvinist press he had won but he had not 'played the game'.

The grimness of the First World War gave Scott's tragic expedition and Oates's self-sacrifice a further, deeper significance. Their unseen battle and ultimate death in the unsullied white wastes of Antarctica seemed comfortingly pure amid doubts about what the pain, mud and blood of the trenches were achieving. Shackleton's *Endurance* expedition, which set out in 1914, was similarly seized on by the press. Reports of his progress and even subsequent fears for his life were a welcome distraction from worrying news from the Front. By 1915 the papers were attracting their readers' attention with such headlines as 'Bad News from the Antarctic' and 'Shackleton's Plight'. News of his survival reached Britain on the day of the Battle of Jutland. At a time when millions had already died, the public were cheered to learn that, despite appalling odds, Shackleton had not lost a single man. The news transcended national barriers: even the German press commented favourably. As with Scott's last expedition, one of the most powerful heroic images was the gradual focusing down of the story onto the leader. First Shackleton had all his men with him, then he took only five on the boat journey from Elephant Island to South Georgia.

Finally, he led just two companions over the mountains and ice of South Georgia to find help.

As generations passed, the circumstances of Scott's death and his extraordinary gift as a writer established him, rather than Shackleton, as the leading national hero until the reassessments of the 1960s and 1970s. Shackleton has now emerged alongside him as, perhaps, a more 'modern' hero – an inspirational leader with shrewd judgement and the common touch. His comment that he turned back from the Pole in 1909 out of a belief that his wife would rather be married to a live donkey than a dead lion is telling. So are some of his decisions, like jettisoning the team's sleeping bags when they set out across South Georgia. He was a brilliant calculator of risk and it is easy to see why so many management consultants today use him as a case study in courses about risk and crisis management, and leadership skills. He did not allow his feelings to upset his judgement, as Scott did when he decided to take four not three men with him to the Pole. Amundsen, too, seems in tune with our own time. His organisational skills, logical mind and strong focus are qualities we value and admire today. And it should not be forgotten that Amundsen was first to the Pole, but that this was also just one achievement in a remarkable exploration career.

Perceptions of heroism vary across generations. What seems to be determination in one age can appear as obsession in another, self-sacrifice can appear to be self-indulgence or even self-destruction, optimism becomes rashness, and bravery just foolhardiness. Scott, Shackleton and Amundsen were all physically strong, brave and undoubted 'heroes'. However, from our perspective today we can see how part of Scott's heroism – his successful struggle to master his own weaknesses – remained hidden, Amundsen's achievement was denigrated and Shackleton's spectacular contribution for a while overshadowed. The passing of time brings greater clarity and objectivity, though it can also make us more critical and suspicious of the 'heroes' of earlier times. But the story of the race for the South Pole transcends this: it has an extraordinary, universal power and rightly moves us still.

THE RACE TO THE POLE

4

by Pieter van der Merwe

Exploration of the Arctic and Antarctic in the hundred years before the First World War involved similar risks and many of the same people. There was also a broad distinction between two types of expedition, irrespective of which Pole it was. The first, dominated by the British, involved largely official naval parties, heavily manned and well equipped, with a generally scientific and geographical motive. They often made arduous overland journeys, largely man-hauling their sledges, which became a British orthodoxy. Some casualties usually resulted, although the loss of Franklin's expedition was exceptional. The second was the speculative hunting operations of whalers or sealers. These arrived in the Antarctic with experience of Arctic conditions and sometimes a non-commercial leavening of private scientific interest. While the Enderbys best represent the British involvement in such activity up to the 1840s (see page 24), by the 1890s it was the Norwegians for whom it was a more significant national business. Generally, this type of foray attempted little or no land travel, for obvious reasons.

In between the Enderbys and the Norwegians, there were also other scientific expeditions, with or without some level of naval support. At the same time as the *Discovery* was preparing to head south, so too were a German party under Professor von Drygalski; Swedish and French parties to Graham Land on the Antarctic Peninsula under Dr Otto Nordenskjöld and Dr JB Charcot respectively; and another to the Weddell Sea under the experienced Scottish naturalist and explorer Dr William S Bruce. While both the *Discovery* and *Nimrod* expeditions fell into this bracket, the former was Royal Naval in its approach, scale and methods, whereas the latter had much in common with de Gerlache's equally hand-to-mouth and romantically motivated *Belgica* venture (see page 28), though it achieved much more.

Scott represents the end of a long tradition of Royal Naval officers who took up polar exploration primarily as a means of advancing their careers, and he might have retired as an admiral had he not died as a result. Albeit not a commercial voyager in the whalers' sense, Shackleton was no less a career seaman seeking the rewards of enterprise, though he showed no gift for accumulating fortune. He, too, went to the Antarctic by chance, caught the polar 'bug' and aimed to exploit his success as an explorer, both financially and for new projects as an early example of a 'media celebrity'. His personality and presentational skills were much more suited to this than either Amundsen's or Scott's (though

Fram **was specially designed** for Nansen's 1893–1896 Arctic polar-drift expedition, then reused for Sverdrup's 1898–1902 Canadian Arctic expedition. Neglected for years after Amundsen's Antarctic expedition, she eventually became a museum ship in 1936.

Scott was the best writer), and the fact that he was knighted on his return in 1909 was partly a recognition of his success as a public figure as well as his achievements as an explorer. The acclaim that his 'near-miss' at the South Pole garnered, in the year that also saw the North Pole reached, put polar exploration back on the British public agenda.

Fram, 1910–1912

Neither Scott nor Shackleton came from a 'cold-climate' background, which was a disadvantage on both a personal and technical level. More insidious was the varying degree to which they took the superiority of established British naval methods for granted, superficially absorbing foreign equipment improvements but not the underlying advances

Roald Amundsen in his garden at Bundefjord with his dog, Rex, before his south-polar expedition. *Fram*, borrowed from the Norwegian state, is anchored in the background. Photograph by Anders Wilse, 1910. ABOVE

in approach. Their insular aversion to using sledge dogs was a prime example, compounded by the error of substituting ponies without well-proved reason. Shackleton at least learned that these were mistakes, though only fully so after Amundsen's success: Scott repeated them and paid a heavy price. It is ironic, however, that he and Shackleton – not Amundsen – saw that the future lay with motorised transport, ineffective as their pioneering attempts to use it were.

As a Norwegian, Amundsen came from a different tradition and a country that in around 1900 had a population of under two million – one tenth of Britain's. Here, individualistic merchant seafaring and whaling, untainted by British social contempt for 'trade', were a dominant commercial expression of a sub-arctic climate and a circumscribed, clannish, non-industrial and certainly non-imperial society. No less patriotic than Scott or Shackleton, Amundsen had a very different and modern example before him. This was Dr Fridtjof Nansen, who had shown how someone from such a culture might become a figure of world repute through Arctic discovery and thereby enhance the prestige of their small nation. From the beginning, Amundsen made this his goal, by becoming a professional polar explorer in a way that Scott, Shackleton and most of their forebears were not. His success lay in methodical analysis and adoption of relevant experience and skills from whatever source, meticulous planning, and a reliance on hand-picked small teams rather than large, heterogeneous and heavily resourced parties.

Roald Amundsen was born on 16 July 1872 near Christiania, which became Norway's capital, Oslo, after her independence from Sweden in 1905. He grew up on the forested edge of the city but spent much of his childhood alongside his cousins on their adjoining country homes near the port of Sarpsborg. His father and uncles were shipowners and masters there, though his father died when he was 14, in 1886. The following year he was enthralled by Sir John Franklin's accounts of his overland expeditions of 1819–1822 in the North American Arctic, and in 1888 was even more inspired by the Norwegian first crossing of the Greenland ice cap. This was led by Nansen, a marine biologist and already an explorer of note, and laid the foundations

Dr Fridtjof Nansen at Cape Flora, Franz Josef archipelago, having attained a furthest point north, June 1896. Nansen was a much-consulted authority on polar expeditions by both Amundsen and Scott. Photograph by Frederick Jackson. OPPOSITE

of Norway's success in polar discovery, using a small, lightly equipped and fast-moving party, on skis and with much improved sledges of Nansen's design. Scott took Nansen sledges on both the *Discovery* and *Terra Nova* expeditions. Thereafter, Amundsen devoted himself to the energetic improvement of his own skiing, including arduous and later risky treks in Norway.

Like Shackleton, he was a poor scholar but on matriculation in 1890 he followed his mother's wishes and began to train as a doctor. Exploration, however, strengthened its hold on his interests. In February 1893 he attended a lecture by Eivind Astrup, who had been with the indefatigable American Robert Peary on his second Greenland expedition in 1891–1892, and who recounted their experience of learning polar techniques from Inuit, especially driving sledge dogs and building igloos. The use of dogs was itself then barely known in Norway and the idea that 'primitives' like Inuit might have something to teach Europeans was also novel. Amundsen, however, had an open and retentive mind and a great capacity to grasp and build on essentials.

> *Amundsen regretted the deliberate killing of his dogs, even though they were key to his success: 'It was my only dark memory from down there, that my lovely animals were destroyed.'*

His future crystallised that year. Early in June he failed his exams, just before seeing Nansen in his new ship *Fram* ('Forward') sail on his greatest expedition to drift with the pack ice across the Arctic Ocean and make an epic sledge assault on the North Pole. Soon afterwards, in September 1893, Amundsen lost his mother. They had not been close and, with a useful inheritance, he abandoned medicine to pursue his own direction. He immediately attempted to join a Norwegian expedition to Spitsbergen and made enquiries about the British one under Jackson to Franz Josef Land. The latter was to be Nansen's fortuitous salvation when he miraculously emerged on foot in Franz Josef Land in 1896, being fortunate in finding the Jackson-Harmsworth party there. The *Fram* reappeared independently and equally unscathed in Norway a week after him.

Amundsen's applications came to nothing but showed that he recognised the essential requirements. Over the next few years he became both an experienced mountain skier and a seaman, through embarking on a series of voyages on sealers. In 1895 he gained his mate's certificate and the following year volunteered to be an unpaid second mate on de Gerlache's private Belgian Antarctic expedition in the *Belgica*. This sailed in June 1897 and, after its long imprisonment in the southern ice, returned in 1899. It was a voyage on which Amundsen learnt a great deal about the behaviour of men under prolonged stress, and (at second-hand) more about Greenland Inuit practice. The voyage's American doctor, Frederick Cook, had been with Peary in Greenland. He and Amundsen found common interests in perfecting equipment and techniques, while others (including de Gerlache) became depressed and in some cases insane under the constant threat that the ship, an old sealer, would be crushed beneath them. Cook was also a believer in the power of fresh meat to ward off scurvy – a point proved when one man died from the disease after refusing to eat seal or penguin.

A Norwegian ensign, possibly from the *Fram*, flown at the South Pole. Symbolically, for a newly independent country, it was an important statement to the world.

On returning home, Amundsen went back to sea to earn a master's certificate and in 1900 bought the 47-ton sloop *Gjøa*, with which he made a sealing voyage to the Barents Sea to gain experience in polar navigation. He had then already formed a plan to be the first man to sail completely through the North-West Passage and re-establish the shifting position of the North Magnetic Pole, having also learned that a scientific rationale was the only way to gain financial backing for exploration. In fact, for technical reasons, he missed the Magnetic Pole by some 48km (30 miles). However, the transit of the Passage with a party of six in the *Gjøa*, which took from 1903 to 1906, was otherwise a triumphant success. In particular, he established good relations with the Inuit and gained a huge amount of knowledge from them about everything polar, from the virtues of native fur clothing to the building of igloos and the driving of sledge dogs. In this, one of his seaman companions, Helmer Hanssen, became an expert. The long voyage also established him as a successful leader and a figure to be reckoned with internationally in the polar field.

The sledge compass used by Amundsen to reach the South Pole. His team spent two days taking position measurements to ensure there was no dispute of their success.

In February 1907 Amundsen was at the Royal Geographical Society in London with Nansen, as Norway's resident minister there, to lecture on the *Gjøa* voyage. Shackleton was also present on his own business. He had just secured Beardmore's backing for the *Nimrod* voyage, which was announced the next day, and was about to find out that Scott was already thinking of a new Antarctic voyage.

Amundsen himself had also come to London to ask Nansen for the loan of *Fram* for a new expedition. Peary had so far failed to reach the North Pole on several land-based attempts. Amundsen's aim now, starting in 1910, was to pass through the Bering Strait from San Francisco and drift for four or five years with the ice as Nansen had done, with the aim of being the first there. Nansen eventually agreed and, though fundraising proved a major difficulty, all was progressing when in early September 1909 news broke that both Cook – Amundsen's old shipmate – and then Peary (on his sixth attempt) had independently achieved the North Pole. The former claimed to have done so in April 1908, the latter on 6 April 1909. Peary immediately challenged Cook's claim, which was later discounted, though his own has also been doubted.

For Amundsen, however, it did not matter. He would not be the first and that left only one course. By the time Scott's proposal for what would be his last expedition was announced in *The Times* on 13 September 1909, Amundsen had already visited Copenhagen, ostensibly to meet Cook, but also to order sufficient dogs and Inuit furs there from northern Greenland, with the South Pole now his prime objective. Given that all his backing – including the Norwegian government – was for a northern voyage, he told no one of his change of plan, including those who sailed with him, until it was unavoidable. When he finally announced his intentions from Madeira, *Fram*'s last port of call before the Ross Sea, he also explained the change as an addition rather than an alternative to his northern project. *Fram* had to sail round Cape Horn to Alaska and his South Polar assault was to be a diversion on the way. As for Scott, when he had visited Norway in March 1910 and sought a meeting, Amundsen deliberately avoided him and they never met in person.

Amundsen sailed in *Fram* on 9 August 1910 from Kristiansand, after an extensive Atlantic work-up cruise, with 97 top-class Inuit dogs and two expert Norwegian drivers among his crew, one being Hanssen. Every detail of his programme, equipment and supplies had been minutely prepared for the expected conditions and nearly all his men were individually recruited for their relevant skills and ability to operate as a team under his unquestioned leadership. His intention was to set up a base where he and nine men could winter, on the Barrier in Shackleton's Bay of Whales, sending *Fram* away on an oceanographic cruise based on Buenos Aires. Most would then make a rapid, depot-based dog and ski

Inspired by his time living with the Inuit during the *Gjøa* North-West Passage expedition, 1903–1906, Amundsen used wolf-fur jackets and trousers in the Antarctic. They suited his use of skis and dog-drawn sledges.

Blanket No. 1.

Indenlandsk Taxt:

1. **Almindelige Telegrammer**: 50 Øre for 10 Ord og 5 Øre for hvert Ord mere. Ord over 15 indtil 30 Bogstaver eller Tal over 5 indtil 10 Zifre regnes for 2 Ord o. s. v. Sprogstridige Ordsammensætninger tilstedes ikke.
2. **Lokaltelegrammer**: Halvdelen af den almindelige Taxt med Afrunding opad til med 5 deleligt Tal.
3. **Iltelegrammer**: Tredobbelt Taxt; betegnes ved (D) foran Adressen.
4. **Telefonering af Telegrammer**: (Ved enkelte Stationer).
   a. Med Aarsabonnement: For indtil 200 Telegrammer (afsendte og ankomne) 10 Øre pr. Telegram og for hvert Telegram udover dette Antal 5 Øre. Mindste Afgift pr. Aar Kr. 10.00. Ankomne Telegrammer kan ogsaa erholdes telefoneret gratis efter nærmere Aftale med Telegrafkontoret.
   b. Uden Abonnement: 20 Øre pr. Telegram.
5. **Flere Adressater**: 25 Øre (Iltelegr. 75 Øre) pr. 100 Ord for hver Extraudskrift. (Tmx) foran Adressen, hvor x betegner Antallet af Adresser.
6. **Viderebefordring**: (Post): 10 Øre; rekomm. Brev = (Pr.): 20 Øre; Expresse (Xp): 30 Øre pr. Kilom.

Angivelser som:
(Rp) eller Svar betalt, Post eller Post betalt, (Pr) eller Post rekommanderet, (Xp) eller Expresse betalt sættes foran Adressen; Forkortelserne taxeres for et Ord.

Afsenderens Adresse:

NB! Gjælder kun for eventuel Tilbagemelding om at Telegrammet er uafleveret eller lignende.
Deres Adresse for **Svartelegram** maa forlanges indført i Telegrafkontorets **Adressebog**, dersom Deres Bopæl er ukjendt for Kontoret.

Thronsen & Co.s Bogtrykkeri 1907.

Udfyldes af Stationen.

Kr.
Sign.:

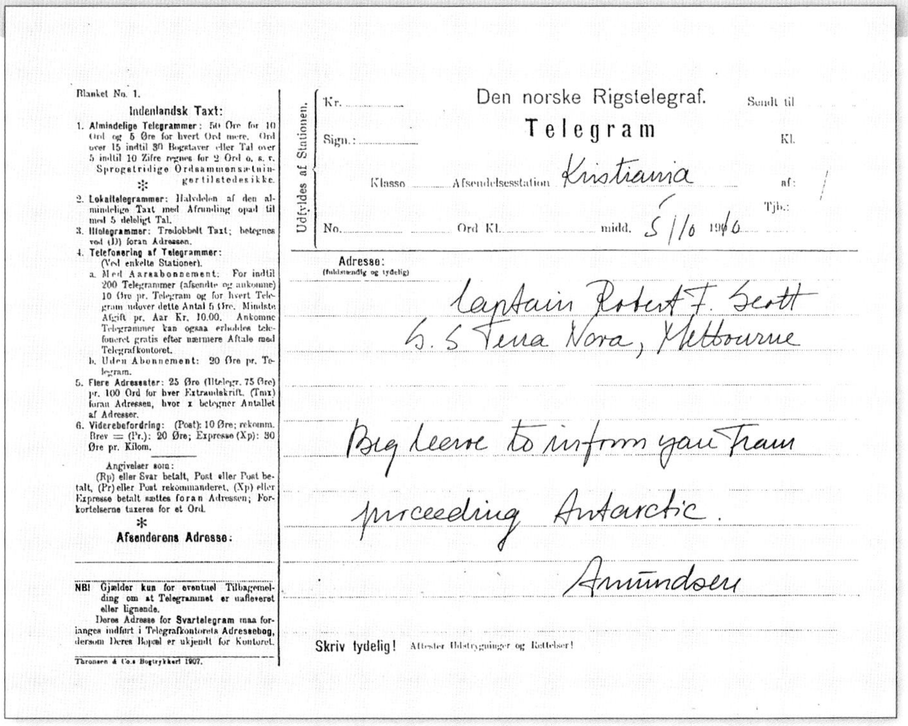

Den norske Rigstelegraf.
Telegram

Sendt til
Kl.

Klasse Afsendelsesstation Kristiania af:
Tjb.:

No. Ord Kl. midd. 5/10 1910

Adresse:
(fuldstændig og tydelig)

Captain Robert F. Scott
S. S Terra Nova, Melbourne

Beg leave to inform you Fram
proceeding Antarctic.
Amundsen

Skriv tydelig! Attester Udstrygninger og Rettelser!

Leon Amundsen's telegraph informing Scott of the decision to turn south for Antarctica. It was met with dismay by many, and was described as 'the greatest geographical impertinence ever committed' by Scott's geologist, Raymond Priestley.

march to the Pole at the end of 1911. All would be collected again early in 1912 to head for the Arctic. Unsurprisingly perhaps, Amundsen first delayed and then never did fulfil his original northern plan.

The first Scott was to hear of this was on 13 October 1910 in Melbourne, where his new expedition had just arrived. Amundsen had overestimated the interest the British press would show in his change of direction: it passed little noticed as too incredible to be taken seriously. Consequently, nothing had been reported in Australia to explain the cryptic telegram Scott received there from Amundsen's brother, Leon: 'Beg leave to inform you *Fram* proceeding Antarctic. Amundsen.' The Norwegians had started their voyage two months after Scott but that was Scott's sole advantage.

Terra Nova, 1910–12

Scott's return from the south in September 1904 saw his advancement both to Captain and Companion of the Royal Victorian Order. His publication of *The Voyage of the 'Discovery'* in 1905 was also a literary and financial success, although criticism of the expedition's home organisation and of the scientific results cast a lingering shadow. Overall, the expedition established him as a public figure, but its achievements were modest and, taken with his lack of charisma, did not ignite the popular enthusiasm that later greeted Shackleton.

In an era of rapid naval advance, with prospects of war already visible, Scott's long absence had also put him behind-hand as a conventional sea officer. He was nevertheless given some promising short-term battleship commands and, though one involved a minor collision for which he was cleared of blame, was making favourable progress by the time he took up a staff job under the Second Sea Lord in 1909.

By 1906, however, he was again contemplating the lure of Antarctic achievement; hence his exaction of Shackleton's

Ponting recalled: 'The *Terra Nova* imprisoned in the ice, with her canvas hanging idly, or clewed-up in picturesque folds, formed a striking picture.' Photograph by Herbert Ponting, December 1910.

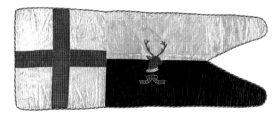

Scott's silk sledging flag embroidered with his family crest of a stag's head and the motto: 'Ready Aye Ready' was flown at the South Pole on 18 January 1912.

promise not to stray on to what he considered 'his' territory – the South Victoria Land side of the Ross Sea. He wisely said nothing to the Navy but gained the private help of Lieutenant Michael Barne from *Discovery*, whose own proposal for a Weddell Sea party had just withered under the disapproval of the First Sea Lord, Admiral Fisher. Lieutenant 'Teddy' Evans also volunteered to join him again and he recruited his *Discovery* engineer, Commander Skelton, who put in a huge amount of work to develop a tracked motor-sledge unit. It was on this idea of Skelton's, aired on *Discovery* and for which Barne helped obtain backing, that Scott now pinned his hopes of reaching the Pole. The rationale was to be technical as well as scientific.

Markham was still influential, though no longer in power at the RGS, and Scott's other major ally was his new wife, Kathleen Bruce. She was a talented sculptress with emancipated views and a bohemian lifestyle, whom he met in early 1906 through his sister, Ettie Ellison-Macartney. Kathleen was more worldly and outwardly confident than Scott, whom she nonetheless came to regard as the hero she sought to be the father of her son and whose success became her mission: he in turn idolised her and found in her a confidante for all his uncertainties. She was handsome, charismatic and well-connected, including among senior naval men. They married on 2 September 1908 and were soon expecting their only son,

> *It is sad we have been forestalled by the Norwegians, but I am glad that we have done it by good British manhaulage. That is the traditional British sledging method...*
>
> **Henry Bowers, at the Pole, 17 January 1912**

Peter, born on 14 September 1909. Between these events, Scott's last staff appointment was obtained partly through his wife's intervention and he took it up on 24 March. This was the same day he heard that Shackleton had reached within 160km (100 miles) of the South Pole – dishonourably in Scott's view, since he had broken his promise not to use McMurdo Sound.

In September 1909, with Shackleton's success boosting British interest, came the news of Cook and Peary's claims to have reached the North Pole. German and Japanese expeditions south were also in prospect and on 13th – almost exactly when Amundsen suddenly switched his route – Scott announced he would head south in 1910. 'The main object of the expedition,' he wrote, 'is to reach the South Pole and secure for the British Empire the honour of this achievement.' Shackleton's own immediate plans to return came to nothing but he assured Scott there would be no clash of interests.

Scott's preparations this time combined aspects of both the *Discovery* and *Nimrod* voyages. Again there was a naval backbone but he had to raise the funding himself, which eventually amounted to around £50,000. Shortening his deadline to fit the southern seasons from August to 1 June 1910 gave him nine months rather than Shackleton's seven.

The ponies, seen here with Captain Oates on board *Terra Nova*, were a vital part of the plan to reach the South Pole. Despite proving inadequate, they exceeded expectations. Photograph by Herbert Ponting, December 1910.

The expedition hut with Mount Erebus in the background. The stable, on the left, was built out of fodder bales with a roof of tarpaulins over rafters. Photograph by Herbert Ponting, 1910–1911. OPPOSITE TOP

Scott's 'den', cluttered with his books, photographs of Kathleen and his son, Peter, polar clothing, and a pipe rack. His much loved naval overcoat lies on his bed. Photograph by Herbert Ponting, winter 1911. OPPOSITE BELOW

It was a formidable task as the final money was only raised in Australia and New Zealand, but there was patriotic support at home from sponsors, who gave supplies and equipment, contributions from schools for dogs and ponies, and a £20,000 grant from the government.

Discovery was unavailable, now being a Hudson's Bay Company ship. Scott instead chose the old *Terra Nova*, the 700-ton Scottish steam-auxiliary built in 1884, which the Admiralty had resold for whaling. Scott bought her back in a run-down state and Evans did wonders converting her but the conditions on board were to be as crowded, overloaded, unpleasant and dangerous as on *Nimrod*. She nearly foundered in a Southern Ocean storm before reaching McMurdo Sound due to failure to renew her emergency pump and the fact that, after New Zealand, there was no engineer officer on board. Because Skelton now outranked him, albeit as a specialist engineer, Evans did not want him included. Scott therefore had to choose, and ditched Skelton. Considering he was carrying the motor-traction units the latter had built, this turned out to be unfortunate.

Wilson, Scott's indispensable spiritual support, had long agreed to come as artist and head of the strong scientific team, which included Raymond Priestley, the geologist from *Nimrod*, who was picked up in New Zealand. Other *Discovery* hands included Crean, Lashly, and the burly Welsh Petty Officer Edgar Evans. Scott was also besieged by some 8,000 volunteers of all sorts. Markham played a hand in his agreement to take the Royal Indian Marine lieutenant Henry Bowers, known as 'Birdie' for his aquiline features. Money also talked: the well-off but unpretentiously spartan cavalryman, Captain Lawrence Oates of the 6th Inniskilling Dragoons, had been badly wounded in the Boer War and, bored with peacetime service, he volunteered, offering £1,000 for a place. Scott, failing to learn from Shackleton's experience, intended to take Manchurian ponies. Since Oates knew a great deal about horses he got his place, but what Scott then failed to do was to send Oates to buy them. This was left to Cecil Meares, a rather mys-

An informal group photograph of the officers and scientists, and Debenham's teddy bear, in the wardroom of *Terra Nova*. Photograph by Herbert Ponting, December 1910. ABOVE

Olaf Bjaaland, a professional skier, planing sledge runners in preparation for Amundsen reaching the South Pole. They adjusted the skis, customised foot bindings and crampons, and altered the sledges to make loading easier. RIGHT

terious Russian expert, reputedly with spying connections, and the only experienced British dog driver to be taken. Nansen had prevailed on Scott to include some dogs, despite his lack of faith in them, and Meares made an epic journey of his own to Siberia to buy 33 good ones – a third of the number taken by Amundsen. He was almost casually told to pick up some ponies as well, though he knew nothing about them. Oates immediately saw that the 20 specimens he shipped 8,000 miles from Mukden to New Zealand were mostly overpriced 'crocks', and one died en route.

Scott took the same attitude to skiing as to dogs. Despite having tried it himself on the *Discovery* voyage, he had never seen effective skiing until he visited Norway to test one of the sledge tractors. Here Nansen introduced him to Tryggve Gran, a well-off young Norwegian who had been trying to mount his own expedition. Gran's skiing – which was nothing special – so impressed Scott that he changed his opinion, decided that skis should be taken and asked Gran to come as instructor. Today, when thousands of far better-equipped amateurs know how difficult skiing is to master as an adult, Scott's belief that his men could do so as part of an expedition in which their lives might depend on it seems bizarre. (Amundsen's men, like Gran, had of course been on skis since they could walk.) Others who were to play significant roles in Scott's team were Apsley Cherry-Garrard, a young Cambridge graduate who also paid his way and wrote one of the best accounts of the voyage; the retired naval lieutenant Victor Campbell, who was first mate and was to command a second shore party, eventually landed to explore South Victoria Land; and Herbert Ponting, the photographer whose stills and film footage were to immortalise Scott's last expedition in visual form. Scott became known as 'the Owner'; Teddy Evans as the 'Skipper'; the formidable Campbell 'the Wicked Mate' and Oates as 'Titus' or 'the Soldier'. Wilson, the peacemaker, was known as 'Uncle Bill'.

The ship's patriotic send-off from London on 1 June 1910 was under the white ensign, a Naval blessing not granted to *Discovery*. (Scott had been made a member of the Royal Yacht Squadron, which has the privilege of flying it.) Kathleen, with Teddy Evans's and Wilson's wives, travelled by steamer as far as New Zealand. What would be last farewells for two of them took place when *Terra Nova* sailed from Port Chalmers on 29 November. The ship started to unload at McMurdo Sound on 5 January 1911 after the stormy passage, during which two ponies died and one dog was swept overboard. Scott was obliged to set up his camp at Cape Evans on Ross Island, 12 miles north of Hut Point, rather than as intended at Cape Crozier, on the eastern side and closer to the Pole. During unloading, one of the much-vaunted motor sledges was carelessly lost through the sea ice to the bottom of the Sound.

On 24 January Scott led a large party to begin setting up depots south across the Barrier. Wilson and Meares successfully drove two dog teams but Scott remained sceptical about them until their good performance was reinforced by Oates's worst fears about the ponies. As Shackleton's had, they struggled through deep snow rather than trotting on top of it like dogs, and alternately sweated and froze, necessitating constant care: dogs, by contrast, do not sweat and have thick fur. Furthermore, all their feed was additional weight to carry: Antarctica provided inexhaustible seal and penguin meat for dogs and men, but nothing for herbivores. After only 18 days' march, the ponies were weakening and Oates advised driving them as far as possible before butchering them as meat depots for the Polar Party (as it was formally titled). The more sentimental Scott sent three back, only one of which survived the journey. The result was that when they finally laid their most southerly major supply dump, the famous 'One Ton' depot, it was only 210km (130 miles) south from Cape Evans, and more than 30 miles (48km) north of the point intended – the 80th parallel of latitude.

The party returned to Hut Point again at the end of February, but not before Bowers, Cherry-Garrard and Crean made the mistake of camping on weak sea ice to the south, with four of the five surviving ponies. The ice broke up in the night, leaving them adrift with one pony lost and killer whales in the offing. Crean leaped from floe to floe to get help from Scott on the Barrier proper, and his companions also managed to reach safety, abandoning the ponies. When a chance arose to rescue them next day, two fell in the sea and had to be killed with pickaxes before the killer whales got them. The temporary ice break-up also marooned the whole party uncomfortably in the old *Discovery* hut, within sight of Cape Evans, until mid-April.

By then, in late February, Scott received a message from Campbell on *Terra Nova* that he had been unable to get ashore on King Edward VII Land on the east of the Ross Sea, as first intended. On 3 February he had instead found Amundsen setting up camp near the Barrier edge in the Bay of Whales, where *Fram* had arrived ten days after Scott and some 100km (60 miles) closer to the Pole. The meeting was painfully polite but hospitable on both sides, with Amundsen being quite frank about his intention to reach the Pole at the first opportunity. It was clear to Campbell that they were a compact, highly prepared and comfortably quartered group (*Fram* was luxurious compared to *Terra Nova*), as well as impressively fast-moving dog and ski specialists – a small display of Norwegian gamesmanship in this regard having greeted their guests' arrival. Amundsen invited Campbell to set up a base nearby but he naturally declined, hurried back to leave the news and his two ponies at Hut Point, and went on to set up a base camp near Cape Adare before *Terra Nova* left to winter in New Zealand.

Scott now recognised that it was going to be a race, but not how fast the prize was slipping from his grasp. While Amundsen had experienced setbacks, including problems with his tents, inadequate ski boots, some personal frictions and medical problems (he himself was a martyr to serious piles, a bane of polar life), and had also overtaxed his dogs before they were re-acclimatised to polar conditions, he nonetheless managed to lay a depot on 14 February at 80° south. This was 56km (35 miles) beyond Scott's 'One Ton', and was laid just four days from 'Framheim', as he called his base. In the first week of March, when Scott had already finished sledging for the season, the Norwegians laid their furthest depot at 82° south, more than 240km (150 miles) beyond 'One Ton'. This caused some dissatisfaction: Amundsen's philosophy was to include large margins of safety at every point, but their target had been latitude 83°, a further 110km (69 miles). Building up seal meat at the 80° depot on a final April journey, days before Scott at last got back to Cape Evans, they lost two dogs in a crevasse. Otherwise there were no significant problems and they were covering anything between 24 and 80km (15 and 50 miles) a day. In a series of rapid forays over two months, Amundsen's eight men and 50 dogs had moved three times the weight of supplies further than Scott had moved a ton in a single month-long march with 13 men and eight ponies, seven of which had been lost.

Scott's party passed the winter on the *Discovery* pattern. Class distinctions were preserved, officers and men being separated in the Cape Evans hut, but all busy on scientific observations or on servicing equipment. Wilson revived the *South Polar Times*, Ponting gave magic lantern shows and Midwinter Day (Antarctic Christmas) was celebrated on 22 June. There unfolded the story recounted by Cherry-Garrard in *The Worst Journey in the World* when, on 27th, Scott allowed Wilson to take him and Bowers to collect Emperor penguin eggs from the rookery at Cape Crozier for research purposes. It was a man-hauling trip in darkness over rough terrain, dragging two heavy sledges and making no more than two or three kilometres (one or two miles) a day. The temperature dropped as low as -60.8°C, clothing was inad-

Dr Wilson, Bowers and Cherry-Garrard after returning from a grim midwinter trip to collect Emperor penguin eggs. It inspired *The Worst Journey in the World*, Cherry-Garrard's acclaimed book on the *Terra Nova* expedition. Photograph by Herbert Ponting, August 1911.

equate, and they barely escaped with their lives when their tent blew away in a blizzard. Fortunately they recovered it and staggered home in late July, badly frostbitten.

The Arctic winter night lifted in the third week of August and on 13 September Scott outlined his plans for the Pole. The march would begin with 17 men and end with a group of four reaching it. Overall it would be a journey of more than 2,575km (1,600 miles), initially setting out with the ponies, but once they were dead on the outward journey, they would man-haul the sledges and use the tractors. These would pull supplies out ahead, while the still ambivalently regarded dogs would shuttle fodder up the line for the ponies, and then return to base.

Not all was well, partly due to the strains of close living over a long winter. Scott's outer calm and methodical work concealed growing self-doubt about his own and the expedition's capacities, which burst out as hectoring and abusive bouts of temper. There was growing tension with his second-in-command, Teddy Evans, with whom he was now dissatisfied as a 'duffer' when not at sea. Oates also concluded Scott was not a good leader and felt blamed for the deficiencies of the ponies.

Scott's group set out on 1 November 1911, man-hauling sledges, and reached One Ton on the 15th through unseasonable blizzard conditions. On the way they passed Evans's abandoned motor sledges, his group being six days ahead. One of these had broken down 22km (14 miles) from Hut Point, and the other just under 80km (50 miles). The technology had proved premature, and Evans and Lashly unexpectedly had to man-haul from then on. Scott caught up with them on 21 November, and three days later the first pony was shot to feed the dog teams of Meares and the Russian driver, Dmitri Gerov. On the 28th, just after laying the Middle Barrier depot, the next pony was killed,

Captain Scott in polar clothing standing by a laden sledge. His loose-fitting clothes suited man-hauling sledges, being flexible and allowing the body to breathe more than furs would have done. Photograph by Herbert Ponting, 1910–1911.

and the following day they passed Scott's furthest-south point of 1902. The weather continued to be bad, with blizzards of snow and warmer temperatures that left them with sopping clothes and sleeping bags. When they pitched what they called Shambles Camp near the foot of the 177km (110-mile) ascent of the Beardmore Glacier on 9 December, the last of their ten ponies was killed. From now on, they would be man-hauling their 320kg (700lb) sledges entirely themselves.

They could not know that they had already lost the race to the Pole, though Amundsen had a false start on 8 September when he set out too early with seven men and left Framheim with only his cook in charge. A week later, with both dogs and men defeated by intense cold, he returned in precipitate disarray. This sparked a mutiny from two of his party, primarily Hjalmer Johansen, an experienced former companion of Nansen's who had been wished upon him and who had personal problems (he was to commit suicide in 1913). However, Amundsen crushed the opposition and on 15 October

Bowers's sledge party man-hauling up the Beardmore Glacier. It illustrates the struggle to move a sledge after stopping, as they try to reach the tracks created by Lieutenant Evans. Photograph by Captain Scott, 13 December 1911.

set off with just five men, four sledges and 52 dogs, leaving Johansen and the other two to mount a successful 'first-footing' on King Edward VII Land – just ahead of the Japanese, as it turned out. Despite bad weather and some bad terrain he made up to 32km (20 miles) in a day of five or six hours of bracing sledging, dry and warm in Inuit furs. Dogs, sledges and skilled skiers floated over the surface, and the rest of the time both men and animals ate and rested well. Each of his sledges was carrying double the weight of Scott's supplies. Moreover, the margins of safety already established by his depots as far as 82° south had increased with the reduction of his party. They were further reinforced beyond that point by a change of plan in which his plentiful supplies allowed him to lay further well-marked depots at each advancing degree of latitude (that is, every 60 nautical miles). This lightened the load for his dogs and ensured no desperate marches on his return. Scott, by contrast, had assumed that he would encounter better weather than actually occurred, and had no margins of safety beyond One Ton. His man-made clothing did not match Amundsen's furs' capacity to retain warmth and avoid sweating, and his use of skis made them little more effective than snow shoes. Except for Meares, Gerov and the dogs, his men and horses trudged for eight hours a day to cover no more than 21km (13 miles), damp and freezing by turns.

Being further east in the Ross Sea, Amundsen's journey over the Barrier was longer than Scott's, but that in the more debilitating high altitude of the Polar plateau about 193km (120 miles) shorter. By 17 November the Norwegians were off the Barrier on ground unseen by man, with the Queen Maud Range (Amundsen's name) of the Transantarctic Mountains rising up to 4,570 metres (15,000 feet) above them. On 19th, a turn westward over increasingly difficult outlying ridges unexpectedly delivered them to the edge of what Amundsen was to call the Axel Heiberg Glacier, after one of his patrons. It was an awesome sight: not the gradual 160km (100-mile) slope of the Beardmore down from the polar plateau but a drop of 2,440 metres (8,000 feet) over 32km (20 miles), most compressed within just 13km (8 miles). Amundsen took it by storm, using the remaining 42 dogs in relays to get the sledges up, and by 21 November was on top, having covered 71km (44 miles) since leaving the Barrier, in just four days.

They were only 440km (274 miles) from the Pole at a camp called 'The Butcher's Shop', for here, having praised the dogs' performance, 24 of them were immediately though regretfully shot, to be fed to the survivors, according to a prearranged plan. Amundsen and his men ate the choicer cuts themselves, correctly believing it would help prevent scurvy. 'Wonderful dinners we have enjoyed from our good Greenlanders and I'll say they tasted good,' wrote Olav Bjaaland. From then on it would be three sledges only. With these they worked carefully forward through a continuing series of blizzards and an area of treacherous crevasses still called the Devil's Glacier which, ironically, is now known to form the head of a less precipitous ascent (the Amundsen Glacier). By 8 December they were clear, and in much improved weather passed Shackleton's most southerly point of 156km (97 miles) from the Pole, saluting how well he had done without their advantages.

On the same day, to the north, Scott was some 400km (250 miles) behind at the foot of the Beardmore. He had covered 610km (379 miles) in 38 days compared to Amundsen, who had at about the same stage done 620km (385 miles) in just 29 days. On 9 December the remaining five starving and exhausted ponies were shot. Two days later, having taken them further than intended to assist the party up the lower slopes and establish the Lower Glacier Depot, Scott sent Meares, Gerov and the dogs home. Scott now knew his prejudices against dogs were a misjudgement but there were no supplies for them to go further. It was to be a hard journey on short rations, both for Meares and for the last support party who were to follow from the top of the Glacier. Between the appropriately named 'Shambles' depot of pony meat below it and One Ton at 79° 28.5' south – a distance of more than 640km (400 miles) – Scott had placed just two others. Amundsen, by contrast, had six, one at every degree of latitude back to 80° south, and only a little further between the last of these and Framheim.

With the dogs gone, the British party was man-hauling alone on a slope up to nearly 2,740 metres (9,000 feet). This meant 91kg (200 pounds) a man on their waist-harnesses, with the sledges having to be painfully jerked free from deep snow or because their runners froze rapidly to the surface every time they stopped. With all the ponies gone, this was the price of Scott's 'fine conception' of facing 'hardships, dangers and difficulties with their own unaided efforts' rather than using dogs. Bowers, who had welcomed the idea of man-haulage as a 'fine thing' that would disprove 'the supposed decadence of the British race' now found it 'the most backbreaking work I have ever come up against'. Scott had now learned that sledges could be pulled with skis on, and that this increased safety when travelling over crevassed areas. Sometimes using them, and sometimes not, he set a punishing pace to improve on Shackleton's timings. Near the top of the Glacier, the first four of the support party (including the surgeon, EL Atkinson, and Cherry-Garrard) were sent back, leaving just two sledges to go on. Scott's was pulled by himself, Wilson, Oates and Petty Officer Evans. The other team was led by Teddy Evans with Bowers and the tough seamen, Lashly and Crean. Scott now regarded Lieutenant Evans with ill-concealed hostility, overlooking that he and Lashly had been man-hauling some 640km (400 miles) further than the others since the motors broke down. On Christmas Day the Evans team was nearly lost in a crevasse, into which Lashly – also marking his 44th birthday – fell to the full length of his harness, while making an uphill march of more than 23km (14 miles). The increasingly worn-down party was now being driven as much as led.

On New Year's Eve, to save weight but also precluding debate over who would go to the Pole, Scott ordered Evans's team to depot their skis and continue on foot. On 3 January, now up on the plateau and 240km (150 miles) from the Pole, he confirmed his own group as the 'Southern Party' but at the last minute added Bowers. At the same time he ignored the medical opinion of both Wilson and Atkinson that Lashly and Crean were both in better shape than Petty Officer Evans, who had also badly cut his hand adjusting the sledges. Oates's work with the ponies was done; he was visibly tiring and limping from his war-wounded leg, and he was already having trouble with his feet. Nonetheless, Scott did not question his fitness to go on, wanting a representative of the army as well as of the lower-deck at the Pole. A more perceptive man would have seen that it was only honour and iron self-control that kept Oates going, and that it would have been a kindness to send him back. The reasons for taking Bowers were that he was the only reliable navigator after Teddy Evans, loyal to Scott and immensely strong. However, being short-legged compared to the others and now by Scott's order without skis, he was at a disadvantage for sledge-hauling, while an extra person in the four-man tent added to the discomfort of all. Even worse, the supplies for the last lap were calculated based on only four people and the addition of a fifth, despite factoring in his rations, threw apportionment and fuel issues out of kilter. The Southern Party in fact set out on a diet of some 4,500 calories a day for an expenditure of 6,000 or more. They began to starve from the beginning, with incipient scurvy affecting both Oates's old wound and Evans's worsening hand.

On 4 January the other three cheered and waved as Scott, Wilson, Oates, Edgar Evans and Bowers diminished to specks on the horizon, vanishing into whiteness, memory and legend. They then turned on their own desperate journey home. It was to end with Teddy Evans on the brink of death from scurvy at Corner Camp, on the Barrier near Ross Island, in mid-February 1912. He only survived thanks to Lashly and Crean – the former tending him while the latter made a heroic single-handed dash to fetch rescue from Hut Point.

Scott's progress, initially fair, was soon bedevilled by heavy surfaces and sastrugi – wind-formed ridges of snow – which made the use of skis so difficult that he temporarily abandoned them. On the 8th the party was tent-bound by a minor blizzard (though no worse than had seen Amundsen make 21km – 13 miles – a day in similar conditions) and on 9th Scott jubilantly passed Shackleton's furthest south, exactly four years to the day he had been there. It was his last cause for rejoicing. Everyone was now increasingly cold as malnutrition and exhaustion tightened their grip, with only the hope that they would beat Amundsen to the Pole buoying them up. The 'appalling possibility' that they would not came true on 16 January 1912 when Bowers picked out a black spot in the distance. It was a marker flag near the remains of a camp, with signs of many dogs.

Amundsen had laid his last depot 153km (95 miles) from the Pole on 8–9 December, heading out well-rested on 10th. As for his outward journey as a whole, his target distance was 24km (15 miles) a day, which he rarely attempted to

Hanssen's photograph of Wisting, Bjaaland, Hassel and Amundsen at the South Pole on 14 December 1911. Amundsen wrote that planting the flag together 'was the privilege of all those who had risked their lives'.

exceed, though his final average was 26km (16 miles) a day. Dogs, sledges and skis all continued to run well through expertise in dealing with the same snow conditions that added to Scott's problems. The weather was generally fine and their main problems were altitude-related, though after they reached a height of 3,200 metres (10,500 feet) on 12 December, the run south then became a gentle downward slope: Scott's relatively slower ascent up the Beardmore at least gave him more time to acclimatise.

On 15th at 3pm in the afternoon, with Amundsen skiing in the lead, his drivers cried 'Halt' and told him that the sledge meters said they were now at the Pole. 'God be thanked' was his simple reaction. All five held the Norwegian flag as they planted it and Amundsen named the area the King Haakon VII Plateau. The formal photographs he took failed because of damage to his camera, and only Bjaaland's private snaps record the scene. Mindful of the Arctic disputes of Cook and Peary, the Norwegians undertook careful observation over the next two sunny days, and fixed what they thought to be the exact point of the geographical pole about 10km (6 miles) further on, marking it with a spare tent and a flag. Here they left a letter addressed to King Haakon VII of Norway with a request to Scott to forward it, thus verifying their achievement: it was later found with his body. On 18th they marched out again. Amundsen left behind surplus equipment with a note inviting Scott to take anything he needed, and considered also leaving a can of fuel. Unfortunately, believing he would be well supplied, he did not.

Despite seriously missing their bearings for a while near the top of the Axel Heiberg Glacier, the Norwegians and their 12 surviving dogs returned to Framheim on 26 January 1912, fit and well, down their regular depot-line across the Barrier. They had covered more than 2,575km (1,600 miles) in 99 days. The type and quality of their dried rations and plenty of fresh meat had prevented any trace of scurvy and the men had even put on weight on the return. *Fram* was already in the offing and on 30th they sailed for Hobart, Tasmania, where they arrived on 7 March to announce their great news, after a long and stormy passage.

Wisting or Hanssen with his dog team at the South Pole, 14–16 December 1911. Seventeen of the original 52 dogs made it to the Pole and 12 made it back. Photograph by Bjaarland. OPPOSITE

When Scott found Amundsen's flag, and then his tent on 18 January, it was under cloud, wind and a temperature of -30°C. 'Great God!' he wrote in despair, 'this is an awful place and terrible enough for us to have laboured to it without the reward of priority.' Bowers consoled himself with the heroic struggle of the journey, and only Oates was sufficiently detached to note that Amundsen 'had his head screwed on right ... they seem to have had a comfortable trip with their dog teams, very different from our wretched man-hauling'. They left a note at Amundsen's tent, collecting his letter and a spare pair of reindeer mitts for Bowers. A short distance away they then erected a cairn

Inspecting the tent left by Amundsen at the South Pole. Scott wrote: 'The Norwegians have forestalled us and are first at the Pole ... I am very sorry for my loyal companions.' Photograph by Bowers, 18 January 1912.

where, wrote Scott, 'we put up our poor slighted Union Jack, and photographed ourselves – mighty cold work all of it'. On the 19th, they marched out facing '800 miles of solid dragging – and goodbye to most of the daydreams'.

It was a depressing journey from the beginning. A sail helped push the sledge on a following wind but this soon became too strong, obscuring their outward tracks and making the small cairns and depots that had marked their course hard to find. Bowers was grateful to retrieve his skis on 31 January, having marched 360 miles without them, but by then Wilson was badly snow-blind and had strained a leg, Oates's toes were turning black and

At the South Pole. Captain Oates, Lieutenant Bowers, Captain Scott, Dr Wilson and Petty Officer Evans pose with the Union Flag and sledge flags. Photograph by Bowers, 18 January 1912.

Evans was failing. The largest man of the party, Evans was suffering most from malnutrition, his cut hand was worsening, his fingernails were dropping off and his extroverted confidence had become withdrawn taciturnity. On 4 February, when both he and Scott fell into a crevasse, Scott noted how Evans seemed 'dull and incapable' as they were rescued. On 8th, after a 'panic' over the loss of a day's supply of biscuit, he ordered a day of relaxed 'geologising' as they began to descend the Beardmore – which improved morale, though it wasted precious time and added 16kg (35lb) to their load. (The samples were to prove important, however, by demonstrating Antarctica's origin in the Gondwana southern supercontinent.)

Things rapidly worsened thereafter, as they lost their way and ran very short of supplies until Wilson spotted their mid-glacier depot. Then on 17 February, after Evans had fallen behind several times, they had to look for him and found him in a state of mental and physical collapse. He had lost consciousness by the time they got him into the tent and, mercifully, he died in the night. The reasons are unclear but malnutrition, exposure, scurvy and perhaps concussion from one of his falls cover the probabilities. They sat with him for a couple of hours but left no note of what they did with his body, then made a rapid descent to the Barrier.

Here there were plentiful supplies of pony meat at the Shambles Camp but a worrying shortfall of fuel at their Southern Barrier depot. Unlike Amundsen's hermetically sealed containers, Scott's had a leather washer through which the paraffin could leak or evaporate as extreme cold perished the leather, especially if the tin was also exposed to sunshine. Temperatures were now dropping to between -30 and -40°C with the advancing season and they were only making about 10 or 12km (6–7 miles) a day. Oates stopped keeping a diary on 24th and Wilson on 27th, leaving Scott the only one recording their slowing progress. On 1 March they arrived at their mid-Barrier depot to find a further critical shortage of fuel, with Oates finally owning up to the desperate state of his frostbitten feet. By 6th he could no longer pull and by 10th he probably knew he had no chance. This was the day that Cherry-Garrard, Gerov and the dogs, after confusion over Scott's orders concerning lookout missions and the rescue of Evans and Lashly, finally abandoned a six-day wait for the Polar Party at One Ton depot and headed for home. On 11th

Scott was around 88km (55 miles) from One Ton, with seven days of food, little fuel, and the probability that both would run out two days' march before the depot.

The bitter wind, low temperatures and their failing strength now kept them all longer in the tent, and they began to lose track of dates. Scott had ordered Wilson to share out all their opiates, sufficient for painless suicide. They were not used. On what was probably the evening of 16th, Oates's gangrenous feet made it impossible for him to continue and he went to sleep hoping not to wake. When he did, there was a blizzard blowing and it was his 32nd birthday. No one stopped him when, as Scott recorded, he said, 'I am just going outside and may be some time', opened the tent and was gone.

On 21 March the last three were some 18km (11 miles) from One Ton, already trapped for two days in their tent by another blizzard, and at the end of their fuel and rations. Scott was now in the worst condition with a gangrenous right foot, and had started writing his last letters as early as 16th. Wilson and Bowers, who were still the fittest, considered a joint dash to the depot for fuel and supplies, but the weather prevented any move. Beyond One Ton, if they could find it, there were 210km (130 miles) to go and Scott may have argued it was better that their bodies and records be found together than lost separately in forlorn hopes. Tragically, had the depot been laid where originally intended they would already have reached it. Exactly when and how they died is unknown but the last entry in Scott's diary is dated 29 March. Even at the end, his literary gift did not desert him:

Had we lived, I should have had a tale to tell of the hardihood, endurance and courage of my companions which would have stirred the heart of every Englishman. These rough notes and our dead bodies must tell the tale...

Outside... it remains a scene of whirling drift. I do not think we can hope for any better things now. We shall stick it out to the end, but we are getting weaker, of course, and the end cannot be far.

It seems a pity but I do not think I can write more.

For God's sake look after our people.

R. Scott.

The bodies were discovered seven months later. Atkinson and ten others had been resupplied by *Terra Nova* and were left with the dilemma of whether to search for the dead or to try and rescue Campbell's party, which had spent a second winter unrelieved, living in a snow cave on the coast of South Victoria Land. It proved a short search for Scott, however, the tent being found two weeks' march south from Cape Evans on 12 November 1912. Atkinson recovered their papers, the sledge, the geological samples and various personal items before collapsing the tent on the bodies and building a large

The Polar Party's tent as found by the relief expedition. 'We have found them – to say it has been a ghastly day cannot express it…', recorded Cherry-Garrard in his diary on 12 November 1912.

Scott's sealskin ski overshoes, recovered from the tent by the relief expedition. Their battered condition reflects the extreme conditions they experienced as the Polar Party returned. LEFT

This canvas bag contained Scott's diaries for the polar journey. The edited diaries were very popular on publication, giving vivid immediacy as the heroic story became a tragedy. LEFT BELOW

These snow goggles, worn by Scott, were to prevent snow blindness from the glare of the sun on snow. The goggles were removed from the tent and returned to his widow. ABOVE

cairn over the spot. A search for Oates proved fruitless and only his abandoned sleeping bag was found. On 27th, Campbell and his men miraculously turned up unassisted at Hut Point. It was above here on Observation Hill that a large wooden cross was erected as a monument to Scott and his four companions as soon as *Terra Nova* arrived in January 1913, now with a recovered Teddy Evans back in command. It still stands, bearing their names and a line chosen by Cherry-Garrard from Tennyson's *Ulysses*: 'To strive, to seek, to find and not to yield.'

5 FOOD FOR THE RACE TO THE POLE

by Robert E. Feeney

The role of vitamins in preventing many diseases had not yet been shown in 1911, the year of Scott and Amundsen's attempts to reach the South Pole and just a year before the Polish scientist Casimir Funk gave vitamins their name. For the avoidance of scurvy, the disease caused by a lack of vitamin C in the diet, explorers could only have faith in the well-known recommendations of the 18th-century Royal Naval surgeon Dr James Lind In 1753, Lind first demonstrated the efficacy of lemon juice as anti-scorbutic, although the less effective lime juice became more widely used at sea in the 19th century. Later explorers also held the near-opposite belief that canned meats, when subject to spoilage, could contain a poisonous agent that caused scurvy.

Little new scientific information relating to scurvy and vitamins, especially vitamin B, came to light before Scott sailed in the *Terra Nova*, which left him still at the point he had been when in the *Discovery*, with perhaps a few more concerns. He had to rely on common sense, previous experiences and reports from other expeditions. His arrangements in 1911 were therefore little different from those he made for the Antarctic in 1901, after which he had summarised his belief in the causes of scurvy as follows: 'For centuries, and until quite recently, it was believed that the antidote to scurvy lay in vegetable acids; scurvy grass was sought by the older voyages, and finally lime-juice was made, and remains, a legal necessity for ships travelling on the high seas. Behind this belief lies a vast amount of evidence, but a full consideration of this evidence is beset with immense

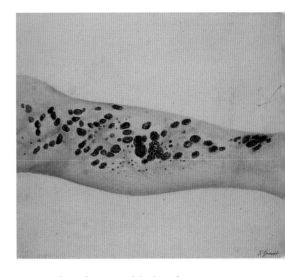

Watercolour drawing of the leg of a patient, aged 50, who had scorbutus (scurvy) of 12 months' standing. By Thomas Godart, 1887.

Abb. 30 (Siehe Seite 117)

A 38-year-old man suffering from scurvy. Illustration from *Kranken-Physiognomik* by KH Baumgärtner, 1929.

difficulties. For instance, although it is an undoubted fact that with the introduction of lime-juice scurvy was largely diminished, yet it is apt to be forgotten that there were other causes which might have contributed to this result; for at the same time sea voyages were being largely reduced by steam power, and owners were forced to provide much better food for their men... I understand that scurvy is now believed to be ptomaine poisoning, caused by the virus of the bacterium of decay in meat, and in plain language, as long as a man continues to assimilate this poison he is bound to get worse, and when he ceases to add to the quantity taken the system tends to throw it off, and the patient recovers. It has been pointed out that scurvy depends largely on environment, and there can be no doubt that severe or insanitary conditions of life contribute to the ravages of the disease. Indeed, we saw how this might be from the outbreak in our western party, but I do not think such conditions can be regarded as prime cause.' (RF Scott, *The Voyage of the 'Discovery'*.)

According to Scott's listings, his daily rations for the *Discovery* expedition contained 243.8g (8.6oz) of protein, 127.7g (4.4oz) of fat and 442.3g (15.6oz) of carbohydrate. This works out to be about 3,500 calories per day. The amount of food (in ounces) carried per day, per man, as originally outlined by Scott was: biscuit, 12.0; oatmeal, 1.5; pemmican (preserved meat), 7.6; red ration (peameal and bacon powder), 1.1; plasmon (meat concentrate), 2.0; pea flour, 1.5; cheese, 2.0; chocolate, 1.1; cocoa, 0.7; sugar, 3.8. In addition, small quantities of tea, onion powder, pepper and salt were available. Scott deserves much credit for his attention to the rations on this expedition. He carefully compared his daily allowance of 33.5oz (1kg) to those of earlier polar explorers, including McClintock (1.19kg/42oz), Nares (1.13kg/40oz) and Parry (0.57kg/20oz), noting that Parry's sledging trips were short and that his party must still have been famished. On the *Terra Nova* expedition, Scott used the 1911 midwinter foray to obtain Emperor penguin eggs at Cape Crozier, on the far side of Ross Island, as an opportunity to experiment on diets. Three different diets were allocated to Dr Edward Wilson, Apsley Cherry-Garrard and 'Birdie' Bowers looking at combinations of fats, proteins and carbohydrates. However, these ambitions had to be sacrificed due to the very harsh conditions. Wilson wrote: 'On July 6 [1911] Cherry felt the need for more food, and would have chosen fat, either butter or pemmican, had he not been experimenting on a large biscuit allowance. So he increased his biscuits to twelve a day, and found it did away to some extent with his desire for more food and fat. But he occasionally had heartburn, and had certainly felt the cold more than Bowers and I have, and has had more frostbite in hands, feet and face than we have. I have altogether failed to eat anything approaching my allowance of 8 oz. of butter a day. The most I have managed has been about 2 or 3 ozs. Bowers has also found it impossible to eat his extra allowance of pemmican for lunch. So Yesterday – that is, a fortnight out

One day's rations for one person on the *Terra Nova* expedition. The rations were divided into standard or summit rations, the latter reflecting the greater demands of the polar plateau. Photograph by Herbert Ponting, January 1912.

– we decided that Cherry and I should both alter our diet, he to take 4 ozs. a day of my butter and I to take two of his biscuits, i.e. 4 ozs. in exchange.'

On 18 August 1911, while Scott's team continued to make preparations at Cape Evans, Dr Edward Atkinson, its naval surgeon, gave a lecture to the men that summarised what Scott believed at the time: 'Atkinson lectured on "Scurvy" last night. He spoke clearly and slowly, but the disease is anything but precise. He gave a little summary of its history afloat and the remedies long in use in the Navy. He described the symptoms with some detail. Mental depression, debility, syncope, petechial, livid patches, spongy gums, lesions, swellings, and so on to things that are worse. He passed to some of the theories held and remedies tried in accordance with them. Sir Almorth Wright has hit the truth, he thinks, in finding increased acidity of blood – acid intoxication – by methods only possible in recent years... so far for diagnosis, but it does not bring us much closer to the cause, preventives, or remedies. Practically we are much as we were before, but the lecturer proceeded to deal with the practical side. In brief, he holds the first cause to be tainted food, but secondary, or contributory causes may be even more potent in developing the disease, damp, cold, over-exertion, bad air, bad light, in fact any condition exceptional to normal healthy existence. Remedies are merely to change these conditions for the better. Dietetically, fresh vegetables are the best curatives – the lecturer was doubtful of fresh meat, but admitted its possibility in Polar climate; lime juice only useful if regularly taken. He discussed lightly the relative values of vegetable stuffs, doubtful of those containing abundance of phosphates such as lentils... His remarks were extremely sound and practical as usual. He provided the value of fresh meat in Polar regions. Scurvy seems very far away from us this time; yet after our *Discovery* experience, one feels that no trouble can be too great or no precaution too small to be adopted to keep it at bay. Therefore such an evening as last was well

Huntly and Palmer biscuit from the stores of Sir Ernest Shackleton's British Antarctic Expedition of 1907 – 1909 in the Expedition's base hut at Cape Royds, lat. 77°33' S., long. 166°07' E. Given to I. Mackenzie Lamb at the hut by one of the New Zealand party temporarily occupying it in October, 1960.

A Huntley & Palmer's biscuit from Shackleton's 1907–1909 expedition. The stores included much tinned and bottled fruit and jams, dried milk, butter, cheese and preserved vegetables in the hope of their preventing scurvy.

spent. It is certain we shall not have the disease here, but one cannot foresee equally certain avoidance in the southern journey to come. All one can do is to take every possible precaution.' (L Huxley, *Scott's Last Expedition*, vol. 2, 1913 edition)

On 24 October 1911, two motor sledges started ahead of Scott's main group, hauling material, but they quickly broke down and had to be abandoned. Scott himself left on 1 November with eight ponies, each with a sledge. Dogs were used, following later, but were not to be taken to the Pole. Travel was difficult: the ponies sank in the snow, but, even more importantly, they suffered terribly as they stood at night when sweat turned to ice on their bodies. Though dogs did not suffer from the harsh conditions, Scott did not appreciate their advantage over ponies. While he knew dogs would eat dog, he does not seem to have liked it as a strategy – particularly the fact that men could also eat dogs. Before his final support party left, Scott made the decision to increase his group going to the Pole from four to five men, which required a reshuffling of rations from Teddy Evans's sledge to Scott's to reflect this additional person. At this point they were all man-hauling, which undoubtedly placed their bodies under greater stress and would have had an

Enjoying a can of Heinz baked beans. Advertising the products taken on Antarctic expeditions was an important way of attracting sponsorship. Photograph by Herbert Ponting, January 1912.

impact on vitamin levels. Perhaps Scott should have followed the 1890 recommendation of the US Arctic explorer Robert E Peary that 'every increase in the party, beyond the number absolutely essential [adds to] an element of danger and failure'.

Yet for a brief time all seemed well. Just three days later Christmas was celebrated with such a plentiful supper that Scott wrote they had eaten too much: 'I must write a word of our supper last night. We had four courses. The first, pemmican, full whack, with slices of horse meat flavoured with onion and curry powder and thickened with biscuits; then an arrowroot, cocoa and biscuit hoosh [thick soup or stew] sweetened; then a plum-pudding; then cocoa with raisins, and finally a dessert of caramels and ginger. After the feast it was difficult to move. Wilson and I couldn't finish our plates of plum-pudding. We have all slept splendidly and feel thoroughly warm – such is the effect of full feeding.' (L Huxley, *Scott's Last Expedition*, vol. 2)

However, the group arrived at the Pole physically exhausted, with their morale further undermined by discovering that Amundsen had been there before them. The fateful return journey started on 25 January. Soon they were frequently stalled by very bad weather, exhausted and barely making each depot before running out of food, even when on partial rations. By 14 February, Scott was writing: 'There is no getting away from the fact that we are not pulling strongly. Probably none of us: Wilson's leg still troubles him and he doesn't like to trust himself on ski; but the worst case is Evans, who is giving us serious anxiety. This morning he suddenly disclosed a huge blister on his foot. It delayed us on the march, when he had to have his crampon readjusted. Sometimes I fear he is going from bad to worse, but I trust he will pick up again when we come to steady work on ski like this afternoon. He is hungry and so is Wilson. We can't risk opening our food again, and as cook at present I am serving something under full allowance. We are inclined to get slack and slow with our camping arrangements, and small delays increase. I have talked of the matter tonight and hope for improvement. We cannot do distance without the hours. The next depot some thirty miles away and nearly 3 days' food in hand.' (L Huxley, *Scott's Last Expedition*, vol. 2)

Then came two terrible fatalities. The first was the death of Petty Officer Evans, a large man, who complained that he received the same ration as the rest of them but that his body required more. In retrospect, one can say that his claim was well founded, although Scott formally noted his belief that concussion from one of several falls may have contributed to his physical and mental collapse. By 5 March they still had a long way to go, but with favourable wind still made 14.5km (9 miles) that day. Yet Scott knew things were bad: 'Lunch – Regret to say going from bad to worse. We got a slant of wind yesterday afternoon, and going on five hours we converted our wretched morning run of three and a half miles to something over nine. We went to bed on a cup of cocoa and pemmican solid with the chill off. The result is telling on all, but mainly Oates, whose feet are in a wretched condition. One swelled up tremendously last night and he is very lame this morning. We started march on tea and pemmican as last night – we pretend to prefer the pemmican this way.' (L Huxley, *Scott's Last Expedition*, vol. 1)

Oates had indeed started failing rapidly, particularly with very bad feet, but by the time he walked out of the tent to his death on 17 March all three of the others were also suffering in various ways, particularly Dr Wilson. On Wednesday 21 March they were stopped by a sub-zero blizzard and never left their tent again.

The last entry in Scott's journal has already been quoted (see page 111), but he also left a message to the public that included his explanation of the causes of his party's death:

1) The loss of the pony transport in March 1911 obliged me to start later than I had intended and obliged the limits of the stuff transported to be narrowed.
2) The weather throughout the outward journey and especially the long gale in 83° south stopped us.
3) The soft snow and lower reaches of glacier again reduced the pace.'
   (L Huxley, *Scott's Last Expedition*, vol. 1)

He also added that he thought they had brought enough food and that the depots were properly placed.

There have been many analyses of the Scott expedition and the reasons his polar party did not survive their return. The weakest link in the end was the food and nutrition. This failure was not entirely Scott's, because the state of knowledge at that time was insufficient to formulate the diet properly. Nonetheless it is clear that malnutrition occurred and, especially with Evans, scurvy is also suspected.

In his dramatic account of the *Terra Nova* expedition, *The Worst Journey in the World*, Apsley Cherry-Garrard stated: 'I have always had a doubt whether the weather conditions were sufficient to cause the tragedy.' He went on to indicate that even in 1922 when he wrote his book, it was clear that Scott's party had insufficient calories: 'Of course the whole business simply bristles with "ifs": if Scott had taken dogs and succeeded in getting them up the Beardmore: if he had not lost those ponies on the depot journey: if the dogs had not been taken so far and the One Ton Depot had been laid: if a pony and an extra oil had been depoted on the barrier: if a four-man party had been taken to the Pole: if I had disobeyed my instructions and gone for One Ton, killing dogs as necessary: or even if I had just gone on a few miles and left some food and fuel under a flag upon a cairn: if they had been first at the Pole: if it had been any other season but that...' (Cherry-Garrard, *The Worst Journey in the World*)

The restored Antarctic huts, in this case from Scott's 1910 expedition, still preserve recognisable brand names 100 years on. Their sense of familiarity continues to engage new audiences.

Cherry-Garrard was deeply affected by the failed rescue attempt that he and dog handler Dimitri Gerov made with dogs to the One Ton depot at the time Scott was still

travelling. Scott had left orders that the dogs were not to be pushed hard and, in addition, dog food had not been left at One Ton because of transportation and weather problems. After waiting a few days, Cherry-Garrard and Gerov had returned to Hut Point. Many think Cherry-Garrard spent the rest of his life believing that he could have saved Scott if he had gone further than One Ton, killing dogs as needed, but this would have been against Scott's original order.

Not only did Scott's South Pole group meet their end in tragic nutritional conditions but his last support party, during their return, likewise encountered scurvy and other serious problems. A look at Scott's rations would not reveal anything to appeal to us today, nor does it tell us its nutritional value; however, an analysis of Scott's diet in comparison with other expeditions is shown on page 130. Although these figures are estimates because no contemporary analyses were or could have been made, they indicate deplorable nutrition. Much of this was unavoidable because of the ignorance about vitamins at that time, but the calorie deficiency need not have occurred. It is also likely that deteriorative chemical interactions could have greatly reduced the diet's nutritional value. For example, data on the composition of Scott's biscuits shows that they contained sodium bicarbonate. This is not surprising in itself, but it could have lowered some of the vitamin content on baking, possibly destroying all of the thiamine. Because the biscuits were an important source of thiamine, its loss could have been critical, leading to incipient beri-beri, which causes inflammation of the nervous system and paralysis, especially of outer limbs.

One of many carefully soldered tins of pemmican (dried meat with lard) taken by Amundsen. Unlike on previous expeditions, his pemmican also included oatmeal and vegetables, improving its flavour and, he claimed, making it easier to digest.

Amundsen's Norwegian expedition was profoundly different in planning, execution and outcome. He had analysed Shackleton's *Nimrod* expedition and concluded that larger depots were needed along the route. Amundsen's idea that fresh, undercooked meat prevented scurvy was a critical point. However, for energy on the long stages he still needed pemmican. A perhaps fortunate set-back occurred when the food manufacturer Armour of Chicago, who believed that Amundsen planned to head for the North Pole and had already supported Peary's successful expedition there in 1908–1909, cancelled their promise to give free pemmican. From Amundsen's polar work he knew that richer, sugar-based foods might cause problems for some men, including stomach ailments, constipation and diarrhoea, all of which could create great difficulties on a polar trail. So he had pemmican specially prepared, first adding vegetables and later oatmeal for fibre.

After setting up Framheim, the Norwegian base camp, on 27 January 1911 at the Bay of Whales, 200 seals and the same number of penguins were killed and frozen for food. Served twice daily for lunch and supper, fresh or deep-frozen seal was the main dish at the base. The men also received cloudberry preserves, which were a rich source of vitamins. Amundsen directed that the seal meat must be undercooked, thereby saving much of the vitamin C. All through the subsequent winter Amundsen's group stored up vitamin C, vitamin D and, probably most important of all, vitamin B complex in their bodies. They ate wholemeal bread fortified with wheatgerm and leavened with fresh yeast (both later known to be good sources of B vitamins). When the party laid their depots southwards, they also did so at good march intervals with plenty of food in each place, the last pre-laid main depot being 676km (420 miles) from the Pole at 82° south.

Amundsen also recognised the value of the traditional Norwegian diet, which formed the basis for sledging provisions: 'I have never considered it necessary to take a whole grocery shop with me when sledging; the food should be simple and nourishing and that is enough – a rich and varied menu is for people who have no work to do. Besides pemmican we had biscuits, milk powder and chocolate... Milk powder is a comparatively new commodity with us but it deserves to be better known. It came from the district of Jaederen. Neither heat nor cold, dryness or wet could hurt it; we had large quantities of it lying out in small thin linen bags in every possible state of the weather ... we are bringing all the purveyors of our sledging provisions samples of their goods that have made the journey to the South Pole and back, in gratitude for the kind assistance they

Skinning a penguin. To supplement the diet of early explorers they hunted seal, walrus and penguin. If not overcooked, all were an important source of vitamin C. Photograph by Frank Hurley, January 1915.

One of the ration bags found with the bodies
of Scott, Bowers and Wilson. This contained
onion powder, which was used to add variety
to the daily round of pemmican.

afforded us.' (Amundsen, *The South Pole*, vol. 1) Amundsen
had provisioned so prudently that he actually had spare
foodstuffs to bring back to the temperate zone as souvenirs.

The Norwegians left Framheim for the Pole on 20 October with an even greater margin of safety in their depot
supplies because of the very late reduction of the planned
party from eight to five. When he reached his last depot at
82° south, Amundsen was carrying supplies for 100 days,
until 6 February, but was hoping to return to Framheim by
31 January. This estimate did not include the depot already
at 82°, plus others further north, so even if he missed all
these on the return, his supplies were still adequate to make
it back with a week to spare. Furthermore, the party also
slaughtered surplus dogs en route to feed the others, as well
as themselves, and placed some of the carcasses and small
supplies at further small depots for their return. On the journey south the Norwegian men even savoured the idea of
eating the dogs: 'The thought of the fresh dog cutlets that
awaited us when we got to the top [of the Axel Heiberg Glacier] made our mouths
water. In the course of time we had so habituated ourselves to the idea of the
approaching slaughter of dogs that this event did not appear to us as horrible as
it would otherwise have done.' (Amundsen, *The South Pole*, vol. 2)

On restocking their provisions they made up their supplies in such a form
that they could count them instead of weighing them out: 'Our pemmican was in
rations of one-half kilogram (1 pound 1½ ounces). The chocolate was divided into
small pieces, as chocolate always is, so that we knew what each piece weighed.
Our milk powder was put up in bags of 10½ ounces – just enough for a meal. Our
biscuits possessed the same property – they could be counted, but this was a
tedious business, as they were rather small. On this occasion we had to count
6,000 biscuits. Our provisions consisted of only these four kinds, and the combinations turned out right enough. We did not suffer from a craving either for fat

or sugar, though the want of these substances is very commonly felt on such journeys as ours. In our biscuits we had an excellent product, consisting of oatmeal, sugar and dried milk, sweetmeats, jam, fruit, cheese, etc., we had left behind at Framheim.' (Amundsen, *The South Pole*, vol. 2.)

At 82° south, on their return, they had pemmican and seal steaks, with chocolate pudding for dessert. Three dogs had died and they had had to kill one, reducing their number to thirteen. When the dead ones were fed to the living, they seemed to liven up. The dogs were put on double rations of pemmican, seal meat, biscuits and even chocolate later on. On reaching the big depot at 80° the party considered that they were 'home' and left it 'still large, well-supplied, and well-marked, so it is not impossible that it may be found useful later'. On 25 January they returned to Framheim with a dozen dogs, as originally planned, and with men and dogs all in good shape.

Both noted and hidden in the many versions and stories of these two expeditions are the dietary reasons for their successes and failures. Racing from depot to depot and killing his dogs, Amundsen did not once appear to be short of nutritious food. It is well known that Scott, Wilson and Bowers were almost out of food when they died, with only a single bag of rice and one or two biscuits reclaimed from their tent. Explanations of the disaster that overcame Scott's party have tended to dwell on the terrible weather they encountered and the vital time expended on scientific observation and specimen collection. This has rather overlooked the major difference between Scott and Amundsen in the matter of food – both in its quantity and quality – and especially so given Scott's reliance on man-hauling rather than on dogs. Underlying this, as we know, is the critical fact that food is metabolised and energy generated by the catalytic fires of vitamins and some trace-metal ions, whose retention varies depending on levels of both prior and ongoing intake, as well as on energy consumption. The application of this knowledge, and that of other discoveries relating to calorie intake and nutrition during polar journeys, was used in ration planning and development for the two World Wars of the 20th century and have also contributed to the development of nutrition programmes for space and modern polar expeditions.

A posed photograph of one of Scott's sledging parties. There would have been little room in the tent for everything, but the cooker's heat was always welcome. Photograph by Herbert Ponting, February 1911.

Sledging rations (per day)

	AMUNDSEN Fram 1910–1912 (dog driving)	SCOTT Discovery 1901–1904[1] (man-hauling) Wt (g)/kCal	SCOTT Terra Nova 1910–1913 (man-hauling: polar plateau) Wt (g)/kCal	TEAM POLAR 2000[2] Royal Marines – North Pole (man-hauling: 113.4kg/250lb sledges) Wt (g)/kCal
Breakfast	Oatmeal (in biscuits and pemmican)	Cocoa 20/±45 Oatmeal 40/163	Cocoa ±30/73 (tea/coffee)	Chocolate drink (dry wt) 60/228 Hot cereal (dry wt) 90/370 Apple flakes ±50/320 Energy drinks x 1.5 c300/194
Supplements	Biscuits[3] Chocolate Sugar (in biscuits) Milk powder	Biscuits 340/c.1,300 Chocolate 31/±160 Sugar 108/430 Cheese 57/±450	Biscuits x8[4] c450/1,728 (chocolate) Sugar 85/336 Butter & cheese 65/452 (milk)	Biscuits x6 55/332 Chocolate raisins ±100/400 Protein drink c±50/189 Energy drink 200/194
Main meals	Pemmican (and vegetables in pemmican)	Pemmican 215/c1000 Plasmon (meat concentrate) 57/c150 Pea flour 43/±130[5]	Bovril Pemmican 430/2004 (curry powder) (essence of beef rations, Brand & Co) (rice – 1 large bag found and 2 smaller, empty)	Pasta carb x2 ±350/700 Chicken balti x2 ±350/700 Beef and potato ±350/700 [NB if these were made up from dry, divide by 3: total for this section then ±450g]
Puddings	Biscuits containing oatmeal, sugar and dried milk Pemmican specially prepared: with added vegetables and later oatmeal.	Other: Red ration 31/? Described by Scott as a compound of bacon and pea-flour. (tea, onion powder, pepper, salt)		Choc chip pud x2 c±150/459 Apple custard c100/350 Apple and rice c100/304 Peach & pineapple c200/320

'...consisted of only these 4 kinds, and the combination turned out right enough. We did not suffer from a craving either for fat or sugar, though the want of these substances is very commonly felt on such journeys as ours.' (Amundsen).

(Calories required to meet physical exertion: 6,000kCal or more than 1,000kCal per day per man – leading to starvation, exhaustion and eventual scurvy)

intake) 6,600kCal

Weights and nutritional breakdown

Statistical weight and calorie information not available for *Fram*

Protein *244g/24%*
Fat *124g/12%*
Carbohydrate *442g/44%*
Other *190g/19%*

Total weight
±1,000g

Protein 257g/24%
Fat 210g/19%
Carbohydrate 417g/39%
Other ±200g 19%

Total weight
±1,080g

Protein 280g/10%
Fat 260g/9%
Carbohydrate 870g/31%
Other/1,390g 50%

Total weight
±2,800g

NB For Team Polar 2000, the overall weight depends largely on the extent to which the meals are made up from powdered/dried ingredients.

Footnotes

1 Scott carefully compared his daily allowance of 1kg/35.5oz with those of earlier polar explorers including McClintock (1.19kg/42oz) and Parry (0.57kg/20oz), noting that Parry's sledging trips were short and that his party must have been famished.

2 Team Polar 2000 refers to the Royal Marines' expedition to the North Pole in 2000.

3 Lunch: 3–4 dry oatmeal biscuits, that was all. If one wanted a drink, one could mix snow with the biscuit (Amundsen).

4 Scott's biscuits contained sodium bicarbonate, which lowered their vitamin content. Curry powder was used to disguise the flavour of meat. Food was half-cooked towards the end. A primus stove was used for cooking, and the fuel was running out. 'We are running short of provisions... as cook at present I am serving something under full allowance.' Scott, returning from Pole, 14 Feb. 1912.

5 Summer sledging supper: 'supper... consisted of a hoosh [stew] made of pemmican, cheese, oatmeal, pea-flour and bacon.'

THE GREAT WHITE SILENCE

ANTARCTIC EXPLORATION AND FILM

by Luke McKernan

In his account of the list of equipment taken on board the *Nimrod* as it set sail for Antarctica in 1907, Ernest Shackleton concludes with a novel addition and explains its possible uses: 'We took also with us a cinematograph machine in order that we might place on record the curious movements and habits of the seals and penguins, and give the people at home a graphic idea of what it means to haul sledges over the ice and snow.'

This is a strikingly cautious assessment of the value of a motion-picture record, and it indicates in a number of ways the particular apprehension over the role of the cinematograph that came to characterise its use in the 'heroic' era of polar exploration. In sharp contrast, just a few years later the words of King George V after seeing Herbert Ponting's film of the Scott expedition reveal an overwhelming belief in the power of motion pictures: 'I wish that every British boy could see this film. The story should be known to all the youth of the Nation, for it will help to foster the spirit of adventure on which the Empire was founded.' The two visions of the Antarctic exploration film given here – one the suggestion of possible light entertainment, the other professing a belief that such a film expressed a special adventurous and noble spirit – were central to the production and exhibition of Antarctic exploration films during the comparatively short period of their existence.

The classical era of polar exploration and the start of motion pictures took place at almost exactly the same time. Motion-picture films, projected on a screen, became known to the public in 1896 and they rapidly spread the world over. Film was developing primarily as an entertainment medium but its value as a tool for scientific discovery was appreciated in some corners in the 1890s. Dr Doyen, a French surgeon, filmed his operations; German botanist Wilhelm Pfeffer used time-lapse photography to record plant growth; Cambridge ethnologist AC Haddon took a cine-camera on his pioneering trip to the Torres Straits; and it was reported that Carsten Borchgrevink's expedition to Antarctica was going to take a Newman & Guardia 35mm camera, ushering in the age of the polar film.

There is no evidence, however, that the expedition's photographer, Louis Bernacchi, used the cine-camera, nor is there any record of such films being exhibited. All that exists on film today is a single shot of the expedition's financier, publisher Sir George Newnes, bidding them farewell – a record made by a commercial film company. Film was in its infancy as a medium of record. Film technology was still being developed and standardised, although the Newman camera selected by Borchgrevink was already noted for its dependability and a later model would be the choice of Herbert Ponting. Most films in the 1890s were no more than a minute in length and thought of as 'animated photographs' rather than as something with duration or great documentary value. A film record therefore played no part in Scott's 1901 *Discovery* expedition but by the time Shackleton set sail for Antarctica in August 1907, the film industry, and more importantly film exhibition, had moved on considerably.

The film of Shackleton's 1907–1909 expedition, when he came to within 156km (97 miles) of the Pole and returned home a national hero, is not known to survive. Although this film only covered activity at the base camp and did not follow Shackleton and his team on their journey south, it was nevertheless a substantial record. Dr Eric Marshall, the expedition's surgeon, cartographer and novice cine-cameraman, shot more than 1,220 metres (4,000 feet) of film (approximately 70 minutes), which was shown extensively over Britain on Shackleton's return, sometimes accompanying his own lectures and sometimes exhibited in its own right as *Nearest the South Pole*. Films in 1909 could now be much longer but, crucially, there were more places, and places of a suitable nature, in which to show them. There were no cinemas in the 1890s, when films were first shown. Instead, they were exhibited as part of theatre variety programmes, in photographic salons or on fairgrounds. As the medium developed and became progressively popular, special auditoria designed solely for films began to be built and 1909 was at the start of a great boom in the construction of cinemas in Britain. Shackleton's films were a success primarily because of his popularity but also because there existed the means of exhibiting them to a wide audience.

Films of travel and exploration were becoming popular as audiences came to see the world around them brought to the local cinema and were told of the thrilling exploits involved in bringing such pictures to the screen. The Shackleton film therefore appears to have been a commercial success (something that would soon grow to become a major consideration in Antarctic expeditions to come) but its value as a record was probably minimal. The public may

Men dressed in polar furs advertising one of Shackleton's lantern-slide lectures, December 1909. In total, Shackleton undertook at least 123 public lectures on two continents about the *Nimrod* expedition.

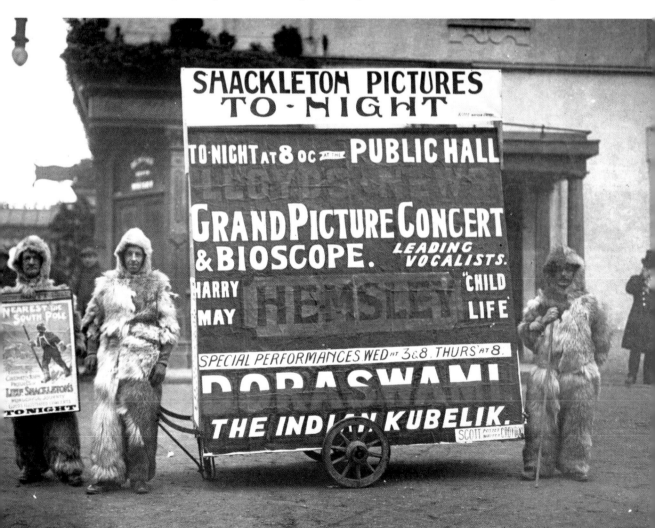

The Prestwich 35mm cine-camera used by Herbert Ponting on Scott's 1910 expedition. In 1924 the footage was used to create *The Great White Silence*, a film commemorating Scott and his expedition.

have discovered the 'curious movements and habits of seals and penguins' and may have been a little wiser about what it took to haul a sledge, but Marshall's film probably had little further real documentary value. However, two photographers would emerge whose skills and vision matched the grand expeditions on which they found themselves: Herbert Ponting and Frank Hurley.

Herbert Ponting was a masterly photographer. His work in Japan in the 1900s alone would have won him a worthy note in photographic history, had he not joined Scott's 1910–1912 expedition, where he was to produce some of the most enduring images of polar exploration. What is remarkable is that his skills should likewise so readily have transferred to the cine-camera. Ponting had never used one before but film historian Kevin Brownlow has given him the highest accolade by declaring that 'Herbert Ponting was to the expedition film what Charles Rosher [Mary Pickford's cameraman] was to the feature picture – a photographer and cinematographer of unparalleled artistry'. Ponting's skill in picture composition was evident from his earlier photographic work, but he also brought a dramatic sense to the filming from his experience as a lecturer. Throughout the Scott expedition, Ponting imagined how he would present such scenes to an audience back home and selected, composed and arranged his material accordingly. Scott himself humorously coined the verb 'ponting' and 'to pont' to describe being 'directed' for the benefit of the camera. Ponting had also thought ahead when it came to his film's commercial value. An agreement was drawn up assigning 40 per cent of the profits to the expedition, 40 per cent to the company producing and distributing the film (Gaumont), and 20 per cent to Ponting.

The release structure of Ponting's films was determined by the nature of the expedition and a need to keep up audience interest over the two years that it would take. Ponting joined the *Terra Nova* in New Zealand in November 1910 with both a Prestwich and a Newman-Sinclair cine-camera whose manufacturer, Arthur S Newman, had given him intensive instruction in its use and had added special ebonite fittings to prevent Ponting's fingers from freezing to it. He also took an initial 15,000 feet (4, 572m) of negative film, 8,000 feet (2,438m) of which he had shot and developed on site before the *Terra Nova* returned to New Zealand from the Antarctic in January 1911. This film was delivered to Britain and edited by Gaumont into a 2,000-foot (610m) release, lasting around 30 minutes and entitled *With Captain Scott, R. N. to the South Pole*. This was first shown in November 1911.

Ponting's second batch of film was released by Gaumont as the 'second series', under the same title, in two 1,500-foot (457m) parts, which were first shown in September and October 1912, respectively. They featured the final scenes of the Polar Party, including sequences where they demonstrated sledge-hauling and life inside their tent. By this time, of course, Scott and his final four companions were all dead and, though their bodies were not found until November 1912, news of Amundsen's success in winning the race to the Pole dented the film's commercial appeal. Ponting then began to devote his life to the promotion of the Scott legend and to recouping the investment he made in 1914, when he purchased all rights in the film from Gaumont for £5,000. This he did against a waning audience interest and much of the bitterness of his later years was due to the public's insufficient awe at the story, which he progressively built up and romanticised, as the Scott tragedy evolved into myth.

The film came to be released in a bewildering variety of forms. Originally it had been three short films, each around 30 minutes long. These were re-edited and released in America in 1913, after Scott's death had been reported, as *The*

This postcard advertised the original 1911–1912 film instalments, using Ponting's footage, released before it was known that Scott and his companions had died.

'Ponko', a toy penguin named from Ponting's expedition nickname. Designed by him, based on his studies and photographs of Adélie penguins, they were made to promote *The Great White Silence* and are among the earliest examples of film merchandise.

Undying Story of Captain Scott. Ponting then constantly lectured with the films, giving a Royal Command performance in May 1914 (where he elicited the comments by King George V, already quoted) and then throughout the First World War, emphasising the call to patriotic sacrifice but now to dwindling audiences. In 1924 Ponting re-edited the films once more as a feature-length documentary, *The Great White Silence*, which followed on from the 1921 publication of his book *The Great White South*. This version, which exists today (while the original 1911/1912 releases do not), was 7,300 feet long (2,225m) – that is, of around two hours' duration – and was released by the New Era company. Reviews were complimentary, marvelling at the hardships endured and praising both the film's patriotic virtues and 'extremely clever studies of Antarctic life', while pointing out that the final scenes were, of necessity, heavily dependent on still pictures, diagrams and subtitles. Scott's adventures were already of another age and the film was not a notable success.

Ponting failed in his subsequent attempts to sell his films to the nation, an appropriate film archiving body not existing at that time, and in 1933 he produced a sound version of them entitled *90° South*, again released by New Era and lasting 75 minutes. Ponting himself provided this film's commentary, and years of lecturing to its images are evident in his polished and succinct words. This time the reviews were more enthusiastic, as reviewers newly aware of the documentary as an art form rightly praised Ponting's skill in it. But Ponting's problem, and that of any of the polar exploration films, was in attracting a mass cinema audience that was primarily interested in the escapism of fiction. Appeals to patriotism have never been enough when it comes to selling a film to the public. Ponting was a great film-maker but he invested too much faith (and too much money) in his Antarctic footage and remained with it too long. However, his film survives in its 1924 (silent) and 1933 (sound) versions and, with the passing of time, it grows in stature as one of the certain masterpieces of documentary in the earliest years of cinema.

The other great figure in Antarctic cinematography is Frank Hurley. Hurley was an Australian who had begun to build up a local reputation as a picture-postcard photographer of initiative and style, when he persuaded Douglas Mawson, veteran of Shackleton's 1907–1909 expedition, to take him as the photographer and cinematographer on Mawson's own first Antarctic venture in 1911. This expedition landed at Commonwealth Bay in January 1912 and eventually divided into two parties. Hurley joined Bob Bage and Eric Webb to secure an accurate position for the South Magnetic Pole, while Mawson went eastwards with the ill-fated Lieutenant Belgrave 'Cherub' Ninnis and Dr Xavier Mertz. Ninnis died by falling into a crevasse and Mertz probably from vitamin-A poisoning caused by eating dog

Hurley posing with his camera and cine-camera. The photographic equipment taken by Ponting and Hurley was bulky and heavy, limiting where they could travel. However, their photographs and films opened the Antarctic to a new audience. Unknown photographer, January 1915.

livers. Hurley discovered all the virtues of Antarctic filming – the tonal values of the ice-bound landscape, the sharp southern light and the exotic animal life – and its many disadvantages: these included the agonies of threading the film or operating a hand-turned camera with frostbitten fingers, the need to melt huge blocks of ice in the developing process, and the constant need to keep the equipment clean and in working order.

In total, Hurley recorded the departure from Hobart in the *Aurora*, the journey south, wildlife at Macquarie Island and Cape Denison, the 600-mile (965km) trek to locate the South Magnetic Pole and the desperate return, with both Bage and Hurley afflicted by snowblindness. Hurley had recorded Mawson, Ninnis and Mertz in their tent prior to their departure but later had to leave in the *Aurora* before he knew of the fate of Mawson's party. Only Mawson survived but was forced to spend another winter in the Antarctic ice, while the *Aurora* (compelled by conditions to return home rather than rescue the others at that time) returned to Australia. The expedition's finances did not allow for a second relief voyage and Hurley's film, swiftly released by West's Pictures in July 1913 as *Life in the Antarctic*, both proved greatly popular and helped raise much of the money needed to fund the rescue of Mawson and his men later in the year. The finished film, which Hurley later retitled *Home of the Blizzard* after Mawson's book of the expedition, was some 4,500 feet long (1,372m), lasting 75 minutes. It was also screened in Britain, thereby ensuring Hurley's presence on the next Antarctic expedition, that of Sir Ernest Shackleton.

Hurley's participation in Shackleton's Imperial Trans-Antarctic Expedition of 1914–1916 in fact enabled it to go ahead. Shackleton was only able to complete the necessary financing when he secured a deal with a Fleet Street syndicate that put forward the money in return for press, photographic and cinematograph exhibition rights. Hurley was an essential part of this deal, as his Mawson film and an exhibition of his photographs had made a strong impression in Britain. Shackleton's aim was to cross Antarctica via the South Pole from the Weddell Sea to the Ross Sea. His ship, the *Endurance*, however, became stuck fast in the pack ice within sight of land before the expedition proper could begin, and what had been planned as the last great journey of polar exploration turned into an epic of survival. Hurley recorded all that he could (naturally, during the polar winter when there was total darkness he was unable to film at all), enlivening the necessarily static nature of a ship trapped in the ice with plenty of shots of the expedition's dogs, certain to be popular with audiences back home. He also recorded the death throes of the *Endurance*, capturing the precise moments when her masts and yards cracked and collapsed.

What happened next says much about both Hurley and Shackleton. As the ship finally started to sink beneath the ice, Shackleton ordered that all but the most essential gear and supplies be left behind on board, as they prepared to set out on foot. Since this included all of Hurley's cine-film and photographic plates, Shackleton thereby abandoned the very items that had raised the funds for the expedition to take place. There was an immediate physical logic to the decision but not a longer-term one. The attempt to continue across the ice by dragging sledges and boats soon proved impractical and they stopped within easy reach of the ship. Hurley then resolved to rescue his work. The photographic plates and cine-film were held in hermetically sealed tins within the ship's now submerged refrigerator and Hurley 'bared from head to waist' probed beneath three feet of 'mushy ice' in the hold to retrieve them.

Initially, this heroic act was greeted with anger by Shackleton, but Hurley reminded him of the commercial value of his work and a compromise was reached. Together they made a selection of 120 photographic plates, smashing the other 400 on the ice to avoid entirely the temptation to keep them all. Hurley then kept with him these surviving plates, his developed cine-film (around 5,000 feet/1,524 metres), a pocket still camera and three spools of unexposed film. His cine-camera and all other photographic equipment were left on the ship. Thus, Hurley's film record ended with the early stages of the sinking of *Endurance*.

The remainder of the expedition – the months spent drifting on ice floes, the crossing in three boats to Elephant Island, the start of Shackleton's boat journey to South Georgia and Shackleton's eventual rescue of his men – Hurley had to record with the little photographic still film he had with him. Since he remained

Ponting filming skuas. Photographing and filming Antarctic wildlife for the first time was an important part of his and Hurley's work. Ponting described the birds as 'extremely noisy' and 'quarrelsome'.

with the party on Elephant Island, he could not record the voyage to South Georgia at all. This made the resultant film record something of an oddity. However, what most concerned the film's backers when Hurley arrived back in London in November 1916, was that he had no film of Antarctic wildlife. As had been proved by earlier polar films, especially Ponting's of Scott's expedition, which Hurley saw and greatly admired, what especially drew the public were quaint scenes of animal life. In the middle of a world war (in which he would afterwards serve with distinction as an official photographer and cinematographer in Palestine and on the Western Front) Hurley was quickly sent back to South Georgia to film the essential wildlife shots and provide other moving pictures to fill the unavoidable gaps in his cinematic narrative.

Shackleton resolved to make no profit from his adventures until the war had finished and so Hurley's films were not shown to the public until December 1919. That was when Shackleton's book *South* was published and he began a series of twice-daily lectures lasting until May 1920, with Hurley's film as accompaniment, at the Philharmonic Hall in London. The experience of reliving the failure of his plans and the sinking of his ship, there on the big screen twice a day, can only have been painful for Shackleton, but debts had to be paid. The film, also entitled *South*, was never given a normal cinema release in Britain but it was later shown in other European countries. In 1920 it was released in Australia as *In the Grip of the Polar Ice*, where Hurley lectured to it as it toured the country with outstanding success. The film was reissued with a soundtrack in 1933 (including additional footage taken by Hubert Wilkins on Shackleton's later *Quest* expedition) under the title *Endurance: The Story of a Glorious Failure*, with a dignified commentary provided by Frank Worsley, captain of the *Endurance*.

The films of Herbert Ponting and Frank Hurley have enjoyed a pre-eminence in polar cinematography on account of the story of the expeditions themselves, the outstanding quality of the photographic work in extreme conditions and the finished calibre of the feature-length documentaries that resulted. It also needs to be pointed out that the haunting qualities of the still photographs that both Ponting and Hurley took alongside the cine-film have enhanced the aura of their moving-picture record.

There were, however, other Antarctic film records made during the classical era of exploration between Borchgrevink in 1898 and Shackleton's final voyage in 1921. It is not widely known, for instance, that Amundsen's successful Norwegian expedition, which beat Scott to the Pole, was also filmed. Expedition member Kristian Prestrud operated the cine-camera at the main base, while Amundsen's brother Leon appears to have filmed earlier scenes. The surviving footage shows Amundsen's ship *Fram* sailing southwards, scenes of daily life on board ship, the first icebergs and the approach to the ice shelf, whales in the Bay of Whales, and scenes of life at the Framheim base camp. Prestrud himself recorded that he also filmed Amundsen and his successful polar party starting out, while Amundsen wrote that his last sight of the companions he was leaving behind was of Prestrud

Amundsen too appreciated the need for film and photographs to record his *Fram* expedition. He jokingly recalled, on departing for the South Pole, that 'the last thing I saw, as we went over the top of the ridge... was a cinematograph'.

operating the cine-camera, gradually disappearing beyond the horizon. The scene must have borne an eerily close resemblance to Ponting's shot of Scott and his team likewise passing into the distance, never to return.

The Amundsen films appear not to have been made up into a finished documentary but were certainly exhibited in

Britain at the same time as Ponting's, since they were included in lectures Amundsen gave in November 1912. But as with Dr Eric Marshall on Shackleton's *Nimrod* expedition, a member of the party chosen for other skills had been handed the filming chores rather than the duty being given to an acknowledged expert, which made all the difference to Scott in 1910 and Shackleton in 1914. The 1910–12 Japanese expedition, led by Nobu Shirase, which explored the coastal areas of Antarctica, was filmed by operator Yasunao Taizumi. The resultant documentary, *Nihon Nankyoku Tanken* (1912) is of greatest interest for its nationalist tone ("Japan has left its imprint on the Antarctic continent") and for taking to trouble to identify each of the expedition members, something not done by any other polar exploration film of this period.

The only other cinematographer of ability to film in the Antarctic at this time was George Hubert Wilkins. Wilkins was an Australian too, who came to Britain as a newsreel cameraman and filmed the Balkan War of 1913. He next joined the Arctic expedition of Vilhjalmur Stefansson in 1913–1916, before working with Frank Hurley as an official war photographer on the Western Front in 1918. Wilkins next found himself filming the misbegotten and amateurish Cope expedition to British Graham Land in 1920 (a short film, *Antarctica: On the Great White Trail South*, survives), before he was selected as cinematographer to Shackleton's half-hearted *Quest* expedition of 1921. After Shackleton died of a heart attack at South Georgia on the outward journey, Wilkins had the impossible task of creating an expedition documentary with its central figure dead before the first reel was over. The resultant *Southwards on the 'Quest'* is predominantly a survey of animal life on South Georgia and, in its journeyman images, reveals Wilkins was not in the same filmic class as Hurley or Ponting.

Wilkins was an adventurer rather than an artist. He would later make his name (and earn a knighthood) conducting the first flights over the Arctic and Antarctica and becoming, in 1929, the first person to film Antarctica from the air – footage that was featured in newsreels. With Shackleton's death, however, the classical or heroic age of Antarctic exploration came to an end. One last film connected with Shackleton is worth noting. Sound films only came into regular production in the late 1920s but there were earlier experiments and, in 1921, just prior to his final expedition, Shackleton was filmed speaking about his plans by cameraman Arthur Kingston for the H Grindell Matthews sound-film system. The film has not survived.

Filming in the Antarctic of course continued beyond the time of Amundsen, Mawson, Scott and Shackleton. Commander Richard Byrd's flights to the North Pole (1926) and South Pole (1929) were both filmed by Pathé newsreel cameramen, Willard van der Veer and Bob Donohue in the Arctic and Van der Veer and Joseph T Rucker in Antarctica, for a film released as *With Byrd at the South Pole* in 1930. Frank Hurley returned to the scene, filming Douglas Mawson's 1929 Antarctic expedition (in Scott's refurbished vessel *Discovery*), for a film eventually released as *Southward-Ho with Mawson!* Hurley filmed again with Mawson in 1930–1931 but became irritated at the short time spent on land. He complained: 'We spent only 36½ hours on the Antarctic continent. To expect me to make a film of the Antarctic in such short time is ridiculous.' Nevertheless, *Siege of the South* (which incorporated footage from the earlier film) duly followed and Hurley's cinematography in it is thought by many to be the finest of all his Antarctic work.

The expedition film was then clearly dying out as a genre and what was to become an alternative use of cine-film was shown during the 1934–1937 British Graham Land Expedition, headed by John Rymill. The extensive film record, some 13,000 feet (3,962 metres) of 35mm film taken by Launcelot Fleming, was never edited into a would-be commercial release but simply existed as a form of scientific documentation, with an edited video version produced some 50 years later.

Commander Byrd and his team had filmed the South Pole from the air but a film camera did not arrive at the Pole itself until the Commonwealth Trans-Antarctic Expedition of 1955–1958, led by Vivian Fuchs and Edmund Hillary, and the cameras they brought now filmed in colour. The expedition was covered in two atmospheric and well-edited documentaries, *Foothold on Antarctica* (1956), covering the expedition up to the setting-up of the base camp, and *Antarctic Crossing* (1958), filmed by George Lowe and Derek Wright, which covered the successful crossing of the continent that had been Shackleton's too-grand ambition.

Thereafter television takes over and the remote becomes familiar. Now David Attenborough has offered us the *Life in the Freezer* series, with wildlife cinematography vastly superior to the pioneering efforts of Ponting and Hurley, and Michael Palin can bring the South Pole to millions in their living rooms, as he did at the conclusion of his popular television series *Pole to Pole*. The original footage of Hurley and Ponting has been regularly recycled in television documentaries, perhaps most notably in the BBC's excellent exploration series based around archival film, *Travellers in Time*. However, we need not even wait for the television schedules to bring the South Pole to us. There are now web cameras positioned at the Amundsen-Scott South Pole Station, delivering constant live images from the bottom of the world for anyone who cares to click on them. The struggle is over but the still and moving images of Hurley and Ponting of the great white silence endure (and the silence of the original films only adds to the awe), enhancing the legends and entrancing us every time they are shown. As Kathleen Scott said of Ponting's work in her introduction to his book, 'the beauty and wonder of them never varies'.

'**Return of the sun** after the long winter darkness.' The *Endurance*, photographed by Hurley in early August 1915 firmly trapped in the ice of the Weddell Sea. The sunlight shows up the ice coating her masts, yards, rigging and sails.

ENDURANCE: 1914–1917

7

By Pieter van der Merwe

Shackleton arrived in London on 14 June 1909 after turning back from the South Pole, to a fanfare of public welcome. Getting within 160km (100 miles) was close enough to rate as a tremendous achievement and the press rose to the occasion. Shackleton encouraged and basked in their attention with interviews and quotable quotes. He was a splendid lecturer and skilfully played to every audience available, including Edward VII at Balmoral. The King put him on a par with Scott by raising him to CVO, and he became a national celebrity, very much in demand.

He was also deeply in debt but most of his immediate problems were solved when the government added to its own pre-election popularity with a retrospective grant of £20,000 to meet *Nimrod*'s expenses. The expedition had cost less than half of Scott's with greater apparent results, and had not needed naval rescue. Shackleton had already started to write his account of it in New Zealand but was aware of his literary limitations. He engaged Edward Saunders, an excellent journalist there, to come to London as his amanuensis, to whom he dictated the story for editing and polishing as *The Heart of the Antarctic*.

It appeared in November 1909, the month Shackleton was also knighted in the Birthday Honours, and was hailed as 'book of the season'. Notwithstanding his shady brother, soon to be bankrupted and jailed for fraud, and his own erratic course in business matters, the Anglo-Irish outsider had reached a point scarcely less challenging than the Pole – a place in the heart of the English establishment. He also undertook a strenuous but profitable lecture programme throughout Britain and then on to Europe in January 1910,

Out of whose womb came the ice? And the hoary frost of heaven, who hath gendered it? The waters are hid as with a stone, and the face of the deep is frozen.

Job 38, 29–30 (extract carried by Shackleton in the *James Caird*)

where he entranced both the Kaiser in Berlin and the Tsar at St Petersburg. In Oslo, Amundsen and the Norwegians honoured him for his achievement and his courage in turning back with the Pole so nearly in his grasp. America followed from March, though more with the intention of raising funds for a new expedition with Mawson to explore west of Cape Adare. His success soon cleared his main *Nimrod* debts and Shackletonian charisma warded off various smaller obligations, in some cases indefinitely.

But like Scott, Sir Ernest could not bear to be without a new project, especially when the Americans were reportedly reaching the North Pole and the Germans as well as Scott were preparing for the South. His own plans, however, were partly based on other business speculations, which collapsed in the downturn of confidence following Edward VII's death in May 1910. As Mawson and others found, Shackleton the polar leader was one thing, but Shackleton the business partner was another. He obtained a £10,000 donation that Mawson believed was for the new project, but it vanished to meet old commitments and though Shackleton engineered replacement funds, their partnership did not survive. Mawson sailed in the *Aurora* without him.

When Scott left London to join *Terra Nova* in July 1910, Shackleton was among those who saw him off. The final phase of the 'heroic age' of polar exploration was beginning but Shackleton was left behind – frustrated, restless, unfit and with his private life unravelling. Emily was devoted and loyal but Shackleton was ill-adapted to domesticity and had always been attractive to women, which had been part of his success in raising funds. He had an intense and long-standing friendship with Elspeth Beardmore, wife of William, after whom the glacier was named. He now began a love-affair with Rosalind Chetwynd, an American who was divorced from her baronet husband and who became an actress. While he still remained firmly attached to Emily in many ways, this strange new relationship ('Rosa' was supported by another rich admirer) was to last for the rest of his life.

When, in March 1911, Amundsen's arrival in the Ross Sea to challenge Scott became known in England, Shackleton refrained from its public criticism.

Amundsen's success at the Pole aroused Shackleton's frank public admiration and his marked restraint from commenting on Scott's failure and death was similarly notable. This contrasted with widespread British denigration of Amundsen and the ostentatious public grief over Scott. That Britain had been beaten was something Shackleton regretted. However, that Scott had not succeeded was a private compensation, not least when *Scott's Last Expedition* was published in late 1913 and, to those in the know, had clearly been edited to put the disaster and its causes in the best possible light.

While attainment of the Pole had now closed one door, it had left open a last possibility for Antarctic achievement. Seeing Scott off in 1910 was Oberleutnant Wilhelm Filchner of the German General Staff in Berlin, who was planning an

Ocean camp. 'This floating lump of ice ... was to be our home for nearly two months.' The emergency sledges are being prepared in case the ice broke up suddenly. Photograph by Hurley, November–December 1915.

expedition to cross Antarctica from the Weddell Sea – a far more dangerously ice-infested bight than the relatively open Ross, and one that had already crushed Larsen's *Antarctica* in 1903. He and Scott discussed the possibility of meeting at the Pole and exchanging men to make it a double crossing from both directions. The scheme was fantasy in the light of events but Filchner did sail in the *Deutschland* and was the discoverer of both the southern extent of the Weddell and the ice shelf that now bears his name. He also found a possible landing point at Vahsel Bay on the east side, named after the captain of his ship who died during the voyage. Filchner in fact got no further than the coast and had another narrow escape through being trapped in the Weddell's drifting pack ice for nine months. However, his plan had revived Shackleton's earlier idea of an Antarctic crossing by clarifying the actual distance involved – about 2,500km (1,500 miles) as the crow flies – and indicating a potential Weddell landing site.

On 29 December 1913, having already briefed King George V and obtained a secret offer of £10,000 in government 'match-funding' from Chancellor Lloyd George, Shackleton announced he would be organising an 'Imperial Transantarctic Expedition'. It would be the longest sledge journey yet attempted and, in the words of *The Times,* would 're-establish the prestige of Great Britain ... in Polar exploration'.

The plan, though considerably modified, was in fact based on one devised by his friend William Bruce, the Scottish explorer. This time he intended to take two ships: one that would land him at Vahsel Bay with the crossing party and another that would take a second group to McMurdo Sound to lay supply depots along the old Beardmore route to the Pole. Shackleton planned to make the crossing in 100 days, using 100 dogs. The principle was sound and worked spectacularly well in the Fuchs-Hillary crossing of 1957–1958. But even then, with the advantages of greater knowledge and mechanised transport, it took 99 days by a route of just over 3,220km (2,000 miles). On the eve of the First World War nothing was known of the terrain between the Weddell and the Pole, and even Amundsen, with dog and ski expertise far beyond Shackleton's, had only averaged 25.7km (16 miles) a day on his polar journey of some 2,575km (1,600 miles). As regards skis, Amundsen personally persuaded Shackleton that they were indispensable to survival but, though he did some prior practice in Norway while testing equipment, including motor sledges, he still barely understood their potential. The eccentric Royal Marine Captain Thomas Orde-Lees – another Anglo-Irishman and the only competent skier of the party – was amazed when, with his polar trek already abandoned, Shackleton expressed surprise at how fast he could ski and how useful it would have been. Orde-Lees wondered 'why he had not come to this conclusion long before and had not insisted on every man ... being able at least to move on skis at a modest five miles [8km] an hour'.

In short, the whole thing was another visionary project launched with all Shackleton's impressive plausibility and talent for improvisation. The funds he needed were raised by his usual intricate manoeuvres, including £10,000 from Dudley Docker of the BSA Company, the government's £10,000 and an unconditional £24,000 donation from Sir James Key Caird, a Scottish jute millionaire. The press was enthusiastic and the scheme caught a tide of patriotic aspiration to achieve some national compensation in return for Scott's heroic defeat. There were some sceptics, including Winston Churchill, First Lord of the Admiralty. His view was that 'Enough life and money has been spent on this sterile quest', with the result that Orde-Lees was the only naval officer allowed to join the expedition. Scott had obtained analyses of the *Discovery* provisions from a government chemist: Shackleton opened proactive new ground in getting scientific advice on nutrition from the War Office, the first British explorer to do so. He also recruited a couple of army officers including Philip Brocklehurst's brother, but the outbreak of the First World War stopped them sailing.

Even the war did not stop Shackleton. He managed to put the whole expedition together in seven months and, when it was announced, he had already recruited Frank Wild, his most loyal *Nimrod* follower, as his second-in-command and George Marston, the artist on *Nimrod*. A host of volunteers presented themselves and the crew of 27 that finally assembled included some hardened Antarctic veterans such as the third officer Alfred Cheetham, who had been on *Morning, Nimrod* and *Terra Nova*, and Tom Crean on both *Terra Nova* and

Discovery. The academics, including Reginald James the physicist, James Wordie the geologist, Leonard Hussey the meteorologist and Robert Clarke the biologist, were all newcomers, as was the New Zealander Frank Worsley, who was to be the captain of Shackleton's ship, *Endurance.* Worsley was to prove a gifted navigator and boat handler. The other important antipodean was the photographer Frank Hurley, with whom Shackleton already had a business partnership. Intrepid, practically ingenious and professionally gifted, he had just been south with Mawson. Even though most of his images were to be lost in *Endurance,* what he saved makes Shackleton's expedition the most strikingly recorded of the period. There

Endurance **heeled over** by ice pressure under her starboard side in October 1915. Shackleton later wrote that 'Hurley ... descended to the floe and took some photographs of the ship in her unusual position.'

were also two doctors, Alexander Macklin and James McIroy, both Ulstermen with an adventurous streak, and several hard-case seamen, notably George Vincent (who was disrated as bosun for his bullying manner) and Harry McNeish, an expert shipwright and carpenter but mutinously difficult. It was once more a disparate crew, which only Shackleton's personality and the sterling reliability of Wild – a pillar of strength to all, including 'the Boss' – could hold together.

Endurance herself was a new and untried wooden auxiliary barquentine of 300 tons, initially built in Norway for 'arctic tourism', though this scheme collapsed. Shackleton bought her advantageously as well as Mawson's *Aurora* (already in Tasmania), to take the depot party to the Ross Sea. *Aurora* was to be commanded by Aeneas Mackintosh, previously second mate of *Nimrod*.

At her own request the widowed Queen Alexandra visited *Endurance* in London just before it sailed on 1 August 1914. Austria had already declared war on Serbia and within days the dominoes of European alliances had fallen, bringing Germany, Russia, France and Britain into the conflict. Shackleton's two army men and his original first officer went off to fight but when the Admiralty declined his formal offer of both ship and crew for war service, the ship made good on its departure under Worsley's command, with mixed feelings among all concerned. The dogs, 69 in all, were collected at Buenos Aires where Hurley and Shackleton both joined by steamer. Shortly after leaving, Shackleton had one of his mysterious bouts of illness, which were to become more frequent during the venture. They also found a stowaway, Percy Blackborrow, who had been brought on board there by confederates in the crew who feared they were short-handed. Shackleton first bawled him out but then engaged him as steward. He proved a valuable addition and was to have the dubious distinction of surviving an operation to remove frostbitten toes, in appalling conditions on Elephant Island. *Endurance* then headed south for the unknown south-eastern shore of the Weddell Sea via the staging post of Grytviken, the Norwegian-run whaling station on South Georgia. They sailed from there on 5 December 1914.

The Weddell Sea, as far south as the Filchner ice-edge, is an open bight some 1,530km (950 miles) deep on the western side where it is enclosed by the

Antarctic Peninsula and about 800km (500 miles) to the east, at which point it is more than 1,930km (1,200 miles) across. South Georgia is 2,415km (1,500 miles) due north of Vahsel Bay and Shackleton's route took him eastwards, passing through the South Sandwich Islands before entering the pack ice on 11 December in latitude 50° 28' south.

This is what he had been trying to avoid for as long as possible by keeping east, but it was an appalling year in terms of the northerly limit of the summer pack. For ice in the Weddell Sea forms and lasts irrespective of season, moving in a slow clockwise motion driven by a prevailing current and south-easterly wind within the western confinement of the Antarctic Peninsula. Ships caught in it are trapped for a long time and risk being crushed in a vast mill as the ice splits and grinds its way under increasing pressure west and northwards up the peninsular coasts of Palmer and Graham Land. This was to be the delayed fate of *Endurance* when, on 19 January 1915, she finished her long eastward arc and stuck fast in the pack ice in latitude 76° 30' south, with the peaks above Vahsel Bay in sight but some 97km (60 miles) further on and to the east. The ice itself carried her further south to 76° 58' on 21 February but then, locked immovably in the floe, she had been swept past the Bay and begun the inexorable drift north on an erratic, slow and uncontrollable course. By the middle of March, Shackleton knew his Antarctic crossing was impossible. The best they could hope for – like de Gerlache, Bruce and Filchner before him – was that *Endurance* would survive the pressures and, perhaps a year later and 1,600km (1,000 miles) further north, escape when the pack broke up. In the meantime, 'he showed one of his sparks of real greatness', wrote Macklin: 'He did not rage at all, or show outwardly the slightest sign of disappointment; he told us simply and calmly that we must winter in the Pack; explained its dangers and possibilities; never lost his optimism, and prepared for Winter.'

In the meantime, on the Ross Ice Barrier, a now pointless saga of achievement and suffering was also unfolding. *Aurora* had been fitted out with great difficulty by Mackintosh in Sydney, for the money that Shackleton had promised had not appeared. The ship sailed in ill-equipped confusion with an even more mixed and motley crew of 28 than *Endurance* and the remainder of Shackleton's dogs, which had been shipped from England. Of the landing party of nine, only Mackintosh and Ernest Joyce, also from *Nimrod*, had any sledging experience and the former was to prove sadly inadequate as an expedition leader. They were so poorly prepared and funded that they had to use Scott's old huts at Cape Evans and Hut Point and had no proper sledging rations. Nonetheless, a party of Mackintosh, Joyce, and Frank Wild's brother Ernest, who shared many of his sterling qualities, managed to lay a depot at 80° south on 20 February 1915 in preparation for Shackleton's arrival via the Pole. After a terrible journey, they got back to Cape Evans on 2 June and found *Aurora* had been blown from its exposed moorings out to sea, leaving them stranded. Mackintosh had followed Shackleton's instructions to treat the ship as their base, retaining equipment and supplies on board, but (to shorten southward marching distances by nearly 80km/50 miles) not at one of the more northerly and safer positions he intended.

It was a mistake based on inexperience but Shackleton also shared some blame. His orders had been primarily to stop the ship being iced in, like *Discovery*, at Hut Point but in trying to avoid this he had indirectly ensured its equal entrapment out of reach, in the pack ice of the Ross Sea. The ship would be 1,130km (700 miles) north of Cape Evans when it escaped in March the following year and in a condition that forced it to make for New Zealand directly. The depot-laying party would only see the ship again when it finally returned to rescue them in January 1917, with Shackleton on board. Until then they were entirely on their own with only the stores that Teddy Evans had wisely left for later users at the end of Scott's second expedition and what they could kill, both for the pot and for fuel in the form of blubber. Fortunately, Evans's cache included pemmican and other sledging supplies.

In January 1916 they made another gruelling, epic journey with their last few dogs to lay a depot for Shackleton's still-expected party at the foot of the Beardmore Glacier, 580km (360 miles) to the south. Its return leg was strangely parallel to the one that killed Scott in terms of the route, deprivations and conditions, and also a tragedy of wasted life, given that Shackleton would never come. Mackintosh's command had proved a catalogue of misjudgements. He finally collapsed from scurvy and had to be left alone, with three weeks of food, for later rescue.

Joyce had then already taken over and got all but one of the others, weak from malnutrition and exposure, back to Hut Point. The fatality was the Reverend Arnold Spencer-Smith, the first clergyman in Antarctica. He had developed severe scurvy and was dragged uncomplaining on a sledge for more than 480km (300 miles) before dying of heart failure two days from home. Joyce, Ernest Wild and Richards rapidly rescued Mackintosh but in May he and another member of the Beardmore party, VG Hayward, perversely decided to return to Cape Evans over the sea-ice, before it

Despite being frozen in, the dog teams were continually exercised. This photograph gives some idea of the heavily broken ice hummocks, this being caused by the continual movement of the ice floes around *Endurance*. Photograph by Hurley, August 1915.

was entirely safe. They had hardly left when a blizzard set in, the ice broke up and they were not seen again. Shackleton never lost a man, but for the magic to work he had to be there in person.

Both *Endurance* and *Aurora* carried wireless equipment, the first exploration ships to do so. *Endurance* never managed to raise another station from the Weddell Sea but *Aurora* did finally make contact with Australia after its release from the ice in 1916. The technology that might have changed the course of events was there but was not advanced enough to have done so.

Frozen in

On the *Endurance* the main enemies were now uncertainty and boredom. Initially the ship was safe and Shackleton took steps to make them as comfortable as possible, moving accommodation to the hold, which was warmer, and transferring the dogs to igloo kennels on the ice. Looking after them and practising with dog teams became one of the main general occupations, as was the care of the various pups that appeared.

Shackleton remained unflinchingly optimistic throughout. Backed especially by the solid and much-liked Wild, he skilfully minimised tensions among a crew that included uneducated seamen, unworldly academics and the oddball Orde-Lees – who used a bicycle on the ice and became something of a butt for jokes, though also a diligent storekeeper and a perceptive observer. People were left to get on with their own work on the ship in scientific observations or dog-minding, but Shackleton insisted on such things as punctuality at meals and maintaining social intercourse and common amusements, helped for example by Hussey, who played the banjo (it was to survive the whole saga, preserved as 'vital mental tonic'). He could control a degree of horseplay, which he often led; he was tactful, understanding, cheerful and although 'expert at nothing in particular ... easily master of everything' according to Orde-Lees. Where

I think Sir Ernest is the real secret of our unanimity. Considering our divergent aims and difference of station it is surprising how few differences of opinion occur.

Thomas Orde-Lees

Scott's anxieties had manifested themselves in silence and outbursts of temper, Shackleton – except when crossed on his known likes and dislikes – showed none, and he commanded an extraordinary degree of trust among his very mixed party.

Their prospects, however, were not good. One of the books on board was Nordenskjöld's *Antarctic*, in which Larsen told how his ship had been crushed in 1903 in the area towards which the ice was slowly moving *Endurance*. By the end of May it was less slow, with the ship and the floe in which it was locked travelling north at about 16km (10 miles) a day, and the ice beginning to work and groan as the pressure against the unseen land to the west built up. By the end of July *Endurance* had a list to port, a damaged rudder and internal structure and was surrounded by ominous pressure ridges. Between then and October it suffered

Hussey, the meteorologist, and James, the physicist, continued to collect scientific data during the winter months. Photograph by Hurley, March–August 1915.

a series of squeezes as the floe broke up and then closed again around it and though steam was raised in the hope the ship might float clear, it was only used to pump against the growing leaks as the hull damage increased. This and further exhausting hand-pumping did no good. Though strong, *Endurance* was not of a specifi-

At Shackleton's insistence, Hussey's banjo was saved from the sinking *Endurance* because it provided 'mental tonic' in the form of entertainment and distraction. On Elephant Island the crew made up songs about each other to pass the time.

cally ice-resistant design like *Fram* or *Discovery*. As the crisis came, boats and equipment were hastily transferred to the ice and on the evening of 27 October, after the stern post and part of the keel were wrenched away, Shackleton ordered the ship abandoned. Their position was 69°5′ south, longitude 51°30′ west – more than 800km (500 miles) north of where it had been frozen in. 'It must have been a moment of bitter disappointment to Shackleton,' wrote the senior doctor, Macklin, 'but he showed it neither in word or manner … without motion, melodrama or excitement [he] said "ship and stores have gone – so now we'll go home". I think,' he continued, 'it would be difficult to convey just what those words meant to us…'

Shackleton's initial plan was to march more than 480km (300 miles) across the now heavily broken terrain of the pack to Snow Hill, Nordenskjöld's old base on the Antarctic Peninsula, where he knew there were supplies, and thence westwards overland to Wilhelmina Bay, known to be frequented by whalers. However, this idea was abandoned, after three days of exhausting dragging only moved two of the boats a couple of miles. Shackleton instead set up what they called 'Ocean Camp' on another solid floe to reconsider the options. They also brought up the third boat and returned to salvage more from the now surreally tangled wreck of *Endurance*. This included Hurley's photographic negatives, which he rescued from the submerged ship's refrigerator, before selecting 120 of the best and abandoning the others and most of his equipment. Kept in hermetically sealed cases, these and the film he had shot were to survive all that followed. With the awful possibility of spending another Antarctic winter camped where they were, they had to wait until the ice either broke up or took them close enough to land to make a dash for it without the boats. On 21 November, the distant funnel of *Endurance* dipped and vanished as the ice gripping it relaxed. It sank rapidly by the head, the floe closing over it as if it had never been.

At Ocean Camp it became a new waiting game, something to which Shackleton was temperamentally ill-suited, and in conditions that could only get worse. Hurley proved ingenious, flooring the tents with salvaged timber, as well as manufacturing a blubber stove out of an ash-chute from the ship and later another portable one for the boats. The drift northwards, however, continued and became more easterly, making the only likely escape one by sea to Paulet Island (where Larsen had found refuge) or, far worse, into the open ocean where the boats were unlikely to survive. At the end of November Shackleton gave these the names of his three most sympathetic sponsors: the largest, the double-ended whaler, became the *James Caird*, the other two the *Dudley Docker* and *Stancomb Wills*, after Janet Stancomb-Wills, another of the wealthy and generous ladies who supported him.

Not a life lost and we have been through Hell.

Shackleton to his wife, 3 September 1916

By 21 December they had drifted 225km (140 miles) north of where *Endurance* went down and were in a plain of hummocked broken ice, mushy under the sun of the Antarctic summer and with leads of water opening up. In an attempt to counter sinking morale, Shackleton decided to attempt another march towards the land, towing two of the boats. By 28 December they had travelled nearly 16km (10 miles) but only after Shackleton crushed an incipient mutiny led by the carpenter McNeish, who refused to continue on the fourth day's march. The first serious challenge to his authority, this arose partly from personal grievances of McNeish and the fore-mast crew's traditional belief that, now *Endurance* had sunk, they would no longer be paid and had no duty to follow orders. Shackleton calmly persuaded them that he had full legal authority over them and that, of course, their pay continued. He took McNeish (whom he never forgave) aside and convinced him that if his insubordination continued he would quite legally be shot.

They were stuck in their new position, which they named 'Patience Camp', from New Year's Eve 1915 until the beginning of April 1916. Seals, which had been fairly plentiful, became in short supply mid-January, prompting Shackleton to save what there was for the men by having all except two teams of dogs shot. This was inevitable but it did not help morale, which was now affected by the lack of food and its variety, and the growing fear they would be swept out of reach of land. At the start of February, when ice movement brought the old Ocean Camp within 10km (6 miles), the *Stancomb Wills* was retrieved and by early March they were about 130km (80 miles) to the east of Paulet Island.

As the open ocean came closer the main fear was that the floe would crack under them or, as nearly happened, be run down by an iceberg driven by wind and current. On 9 March the ice was moving on an ocean swell but though the boats were stowed to get away, the opportunity to do so safely did not come. On 23rd, 139 days after the loss of *Endurance*, the distant peaks of Joinville Island at the tip of Graham Land were sighted about 64km (40 miles) off, but still Shackleton delayed, rightly fearing the dangers of trying to launch boats in a sea full of heavy ice and unknown currents. By the end of the month they had drifted north, out of the Weddell Sea, into the marches of the Southern Ocean. The floe on which they were camped was now bound to disintegrate, food was increasingly short and the days were shortening towards winter. The Peninsula was out of reach to the south-west and the only land within range to the north was Clarence or Elephant Island, more than 160km (100 miles) away.

On 30 March, the rest of the dogs were shot and eaten and by 9 April the grinding of the pack had split and reduced the floe to the point where it had to be abandoned in dangerously ice-clogged sea conditions. At 1.30pm, after drifting some 3,220km (2,000 miles) on their feet, all 28 men embarked and headed northwards through a gauntlet of disintegrating and melting pack all around them. Shackleton commanded the *Caird* and Worsley, as the most skilled boat-handler, the *Dudley Docker*. Hubert Hudson, second officer of *Endurance* (who was weakening physically and mentally), was nominally in charge of the *Stancomb-Wills* but Crean effectively so. The *Caird* proved a good sailer, the other two extremely difficult and the conditions in all three were alarming and unpleasant. For the first two nights they hauled the boats out on a convenient floe. This was almost catastrophic on the first occasion, when the ice split and dropped one man in his sleeping bag into the sea, as well as separating Shackleton and the *Caird* briefly from the rest. Thereafter they stayed in the boats, tied together at night, but three days from starting they found that they had lost ground to the south and east rather than gained it northwards.

Shackleton then ordered a change of course to the south-west back towards Graham Land, a decision that probably saved their lives. For on the following day, 12 April, the wind shifted to south-west, allowing them to run before it towards Elephant Island. On 13th they finally broke clear of ice but the next few days and nights were a catalogue of exhaustion, exposure, seasickness and continuous bailing, especially in the two smaller boats, with the *Caird* taking the unseaworthy *Stancomb Wills* in tow to prevent it from being lost. By 15th, the seventh day of their voyage, with the peaks of Elephant Island before them, the *Docker* had become separated. Given their exhaustion and the appalling sea conditions right under the cliffs, it was a near-miracle that both sections of the party managed to reach the leeward side of the island and find the same landing place – one of very few – near Cape Valentine. That proved to be dangerous to stay on and two days later, on 17th, they moved to a stony, ice-covered beach 11km (7 miles) further along under a spit of rock which they called Cape Wild – honouring Frank Wild, who had soldiered on for 32 hours without sleep at the tiller of the *Caird*.

They had last been ashore in South Georgia 16 months earlier, in early December 1914, and theirs was the first known landing on Elephant Island since 1830.

A nearby glacier outfall offered water and a penguin rookery on the spit promised a food supply; of the elephant seals that gave the island its name, there was no sign. It was a barren, cold and unvisited rock, lost in a desert of ocean, but at least it was solid land.

James Caird • April–May 1916

On the afternoon of Saturday 20 May 1916, three bearded figures in filthy, tattered clothing walked into the Norwegian whaling station at Stromness on the north coast of South Georgia, and were taken to the house of the manager, Thoralf Sørlie. He thought he recognised one but could not place him until the man said: 'My name is Shackleton … Tell me, when was the war over?' Sørlie, who had met Shackleton at Grytviken in December 1914, welcomed them in but had to give them a shocking answer: 'The war is not over. Millions are being killed … The world is mad.' Fed, cleaned up and rested, the three arrivals – the others being Worsley and Tom Crean – had an astonishing story to tell, though one that still had some way to run before its ending.

As soon as they had settled on the safe beach on Elephant Island, the 'directive committee' of Shackleton, Wild and Worsley agreed that their only hope was to seek rescue, since there was no chance of being found. On 19 April, Shackleton called for volunteers to accompany him in the *James Caird*, selecting Worsley for his proven skills, the tough and reliable Irishman Crean, and the two most difficult lower-deck men, McNeish the shipwright and Vincent. The former was essential to repair damage and Vincent, despite his faults, was a good seaman. Also, taking them would remove a potential source of trouble on the island. A final member was another cheerful Irish hand called

The six men who sailed the *James Caird* to South Georgia had a horrific time. They were constantly wet, only slept for short periods in rotting reindeer sleeping bags, and had constantly to chip off deck ice to prevent the boat capsizing.

Timothy McCarthy. Wild was left in charge at the new camp with both the doctors (who were needed to take off Blackborrow's gangrenous left toes) and orders to try to reach Deception Island in the spring if rescue did not arrive. The two other boats were turned over, supported on heaps of stones, to form a hut under which all 22 men had to live, double-decked, with some sleeping on the boat thwarts above and the rest on the rocky, guano-caked beach below.

The freeboard of the 6.7 x 2-metre (22 x 6.5 foot) *James Caird* had already been raised and a small foredeck added. Recycling the timber of a sledge, a spare bolt of canvas and other pieces brought with them, McNeish rapidly stretched a spray-proof but neither watertight nor solid deck over the rest of it – all except a small command hatch aft. He also strengthened the keel by lashing the mast of the *Stancomb Wills* along it internally and added a small mizzen mast to the single-masted lug-rig. Heavily ballasted with shingle from the beach, packed in improvised bags, they sailed just after noon on Monday 24 April. The crew had only disintegrating reindeer sleeping bags, blankets, and the clothes they wore, none of which were waterproof. Their destination was South Georgia, to leeward of them in terms of prevailing wind and current across nearly 1,290km (800 miles) of the most stormy winter seas in the world.

Given that it should never have been in such waters, the *Caird* proved stable and safe but with a motion that made everyone seasick. After a fair start the

The settee from Sørlie's house at the whaling station on South Georgia. Shackleton, Crean and Worsley rested in this and two chairs after their 36-hour crossing to seek rescue for *Endurance*'s crew.

weather deteriorated to a Force 9 gale which obliged them to heave-to for a day, but carried them on their way. By 26 April Worsley calculated they had covered 206km (128 miles). Everything except sailing the boat was done below deck in an intensely cramped, wet, nauseating and uncomfortable environment. There was no room to sit up properly, and with perpetual leakage through the canvas deck, those below had to pump and bail almost continuously. The pump itself – another of Hurley's clever improvisations – also only worked when fully submerged in the sloshing bilge. The sleeping area was in the bow, the driest part (though that was only relative) and the cooking, done by Crean, was on a primus stove using ice fished from the sea whenever possible, to eke out water. Shackleton had brought enough supplies for a month and, as a cardinal principle of care for his men, ensured everyone had frequent hot food or drinks, and that a regular round of watches and rest was kept as far as possible. As before, his calm determination in the face of immediate danger and his solicitude for everyone was their psychological sheet anchor. Ever since *Nimrod*, he had dreamed of making such a boat journey but, though now doing so, he had to confess that it was Worsley, not himself, who was better qualified for the purpose and the better navigator.

By 29 April they had covered 383km (238 miles) but the following day were again forced to heave-to on their sea anchor in wildly confused conditions and falling temperatures, of which the one advantage was that the deck canvas froze and at least stopped leaking. This, however, brought its own danger as the growing casing of ice on the upper works, a foot thick in places, made the boat unstable. Three times they risked lives crawling out onto the open deck to chip it off, soaking and freezing in the same breaking seas that formed it. On 2 May, still wallowing head to wind in icy conditions, the painter parted and they lost their sea anchor – a potential catastrophe since they could now only heave-to under sail, which was far more wearing.

Fortunately, 3 May saw the start of two days' fine weather but this soon changed to a north-westerly gale. At midnight on 5th they were nearly capsized by a massive wave, after which they had to heave-to again, and spent the night frantically pumping and bailing. Vincent had by now become useless and McNeish was suffering badly; Crean and McCarthy remained cheerful and Worsley, as navigator, bore a huge burden, worsened by the rare occasions for taking sun sights in the poor conditions and with the boat 'jumping like a flea'. When on 7th he made them 145km (90 miles) from South Georgia, they had only two days of salt-contaminated water left and were beginning to suffer from thirst as well as exhaustion. Worsley had been aiming for the western end of the island, hoping to get round to the whaling stations on the north side, but he could not be sure of his position. Fearing they might miss land altogether to the north, Shackleton decided to make for the uninhabited and practically unknown southern side. At 12.30pm on 8 May, through thick weather, they briefly sighted the peaks of Cape Demidov to the west of King Haakon Bay and shortly afterwards, as the murk lifted, had the whole towering, iron-bound coast spread out across their track ahead.

By now it was too late to close the land with safety and Shackleton bore off for what was to be another terrifying night. By just after 6pm, in darkness, they were fighting a Force-10 storm blowing from west-north-west, with huge broken seas caused by the nearness to land. They nonetheless managed to claw off to the south before heaving-to again, pumping and bailing through the night. By noon the following day the wind had shifted to south-west at hurricane force and was driving them towards the maelstrom lee shore between King Haakon Bay and the fearsome peak of Annenkov Island just off the coast. Here again they were saved by Worsley's skills as he shifted their minimal sail to gain the maximum ground to the southward. After four hours, with the boat leaking through every seam from the straining and crashing, and the men bailing for their lives, they finally managed to clear the island by nightfall, with the weather subsequently moderating.

On the evening of the next day, 10 May 1916, exhausted, soaking and in agonies of thirst after a frustrating afternoon trying to beat into King Haakon Bay, they managed to scrape into a narrow cove just inside Cape Rosa, its south-eastern arm. Here they stumbled ashore to the welcome provided by a small spring of fresh water, 17 days since leaving Elephant Island. 'It was,' wrote Shackleton, 'a splendid moment.'

Four days' rest in the cove, where there was shelter and driftwood for a fire, saw everyone dried out and their next move planned. The risks of trying to sail round to the north of the island were too great and Shackleton doubted the weakened McNeish and Vincent would survive the journey. He therefore intended to cross the icy peaks of the interior on foot, with Worsley – who had mountaineering experience in New Zealand and the Alps – and Crean. McCarthy would stay behind with the invalids, well supplied with rations and with local game to hand. They had already been eating fresh albatross chicks and sea elephant.

Above the north end of the long bay they had seen a snowy saddle that looked like an obvious way up. This was the route they took on 19 May, having sailed the *James Caird* over to the north side on 15th and upended it on a new stretch of beach to form a hut at what they called 'Peggotty Camp' (named for the Dickensian boat-dweller). The aim was to reach the permanent whaling station at Husvik at the head of Stromness Bay, a distance of only about 32km (20 miles). That was the theory. In practice, it was winter on a barren island of highly

This compass played a vital role in the *James Caird* voyage. Out of sight of land they relied on it and the wind direction shown by their flag, especially when otherwise sailing blind at night.

changeable weather with unmapped, glacier-coated central mountains of heights then unknown (914 metres/3,000 feet). Apart from being physically weak, they were inadequately dressed, with boots whose only grip was provided by inserting screws from the *James Caird* in the soles. The only other equipment they had were compasses, an outline chart of the coast, a 15-metre (50-foot) length of rope and McNeish's short carpenter's adze to use as an ice-axe. They took three days' supply of rations per man and a primus stove, but no sleeping bags: Shackleton planned to do the crossing in a single march, day and night, with minimum stops for rest and food, taking advantage of a full moon. The weather delayed the start but thereafter was almost freakishly fine, though very cold at night and some-times misty.

Do not let it be said that Shackleton has failed ... No man fails who sets an example of high courage, of unbroken resolution, of unshrinking endurance.

Roald Amundsen

Starting at 2am, they marched up more than 300 metres (1,000 feet) across the dangerous glacial saddle and in about six hours were within sight of deserted Possession Bay, the most westerly of the long, regularly spaced fjords penetrating the north coast. Thereafter things became increasingly difficult as they had to regain height lost by descending too soon and pick their way east across a high ridge whose first three passes proved to have impossible reverse faces. As they used the adze to cut steps down the ice beyond the fourth, late on 19th, the light began to fail and they risked using the coiled rope as a toboggan, careering down a 460-metre (1,500-foot) slope to avoid the greater danger of being trapped above in darkness. In the night they again lost the line of their route, descending on the western side of Fortuna Bay, the next along the coast, and having to climb up again to another jagged ridge. Near the top, after some 22 hours on the move, Shackleton allowed the others a brief sleep, himself keeping watch, before they went over the crest and could at last recognise the distant heights above Stromness. At 7am on 20th they heard the faint factory whistle from one of the whaling stations, though still some miles away.

To get round the head of Fortuna Bay they had a short but frightening final traverse, tied together. Shackleton again cut their steps down a wall of ice, with the risk of a slip from any of them catapulting all three into the sea far below. This led them down to a beach by mid-morning with one more 460-metre (1,500 foot) ridge to cross to reach Stromness, which Shackleton now judged an easier destination than Husvik. To their jubilation, Stromness Bay was in sight below by early afternoon. On the way down, their last misdirection left them in a mountain stream with a soaking, 10-metre (30-foot) drop through the waterfall at the end of it using their rope, which at last proved its strength but was lost there. Thirty-six hours after starting out, they walked into the whaling station at about 4pm, 2,415km (1,500 miles) north of where *Endurance* had frozen in the pack-ice, and into a world that the slaughter of Flanders and Gallipoli had already changed forever.

Yelcho • May–August 1916

Although the final scene of Shackleton's expedition was only played out in 1917 when he returned in *Aurora* to rescue the Ross Sea party, the last act of the *Endurance* drama remained a fairly local matter. On the night of their arrival, Worsley slept on board the whale-catcher *Samson*, already making its way out through a blizzard to fetch the men at King Haakon Bay, who did not initially recognise his cleaned-up form when he arrived. They returned to Stromness on Monday 22nd, bringing the *James Caird* with them, a gesture Shackleton greatly appreciated. (In 1922, after his death, it was presented to Dulwich College, his old school, where it can still be seen.)

During their absence Shackleton was also lent the use of an English steam whaler laid up at Husvik, the *Southern Sky*, to mount a rescue of the men on Elephant Island. He, Worsley and Crean sailed with it on 23 May under a Norwegian captain, Ingvar Thom, who happened to be available as his ship was in harbour, but they were stopped by thick sea ice 113km (70 miles) short. Instead of returning to South Georgia, however, Shackleton diverted Thom to Port Stanley in the Falkland Islands, which had a cable station, and announced his escape to the world via the London *Daily Chronicle*, to which he was under commercial contract. The news broke in banner headlines on 31 May, the day the Battle of Jutland was fought. Thom then left and Shackleton found himself enjoying the hospitality of the Governor but with no ship available in Stanley to make another rescue attempt.

By this time his supporters in London, including Ernest Perris, editor of the *Chronicle*, had already been urging high-level official action over the vanished expedition. The Admiralty was understandably reluctant, both because of the war and having had enough of sorting out such messes in the recent past. However, an approach to Prime Minister Herbert Asquith, and *Aurora*'s wireless signal to Australia on March 24 1916 after its escape from the ice, clinched the matter even before Shackleton materialised to appeal for help two months later. The Navy now began to fit out *Discovery* for the task but showed no willingness to allow

Sir Ernest Shackleton in Royal Naval Reserve uniform after returning from the Antarctic. Despite the horrors of the First World War, his miraculous escape was a welcome distraction. Unknown photographer, about 1917.

him any authority to direct its movements. Already fixed on the mission of rescuing his men, he was equally adamant that he should be in overall command.

Through the good offices of the Argentine government, the next attempt to reach Elephant Island was made by the Argentine fisheries research trawler *Instituto di Pesca No 1*. This collected Shackleton, Worsley and Crean from Port Stanley on 16 June but returned them there after being forced back by ice again, 32km (20 miles) from the island.

With only the option of waiting for *Discovery* at Port Stanley, on 1 July the three men shifted their ground to Punta Arenas in Chile, on the Straits of Magellan. Here Shackleton quickly raised money from the British community and other admirers to charter a 75-ton schooner, the *Emma*, for his third rescue attempt. They sailed on 12th, towed part of the way by the Chilean Navy tender *Yelcho*, but the voyage was otherwise more reminiscent of the pre-steam era. It was made largely under sail because of deficiencies in the *Emma*'s diesel engine and they were again stopped 160km (100 miles) short by ice. They then had to beat back against the prevailing westerlies, reaching Port Stanley on 3 August.

With no prospect of *Discovery* arriving before late September and the distant Admiralty immoveable that he would be nothing but a passenger, Shackleton was now becoming desperately anxious for his men. The Chileans again sent out the *Yelcho* to help him return *Emma* to Punta Arenas, where it arrived on 14 August with Shackleton again in doubtful health. There, his burning desire to rescue his men before the Royal Navy arrived persuaded both the local naval commander and his superiors in Santiago to allow one last attempt using *Yelcho* alone. It was a small steel tug of about 150 tons, not in very good repair either structurally or mechanically and certainly not built for ice. Shackleton, Worsley and Crean sailed in it with a crew of Chilean volunteers on 25 August. The commander, Lieutenant Luis Pardo, obligingly allowed Shackleton his head to direct their movements and wisely left the navigation to Worsley.

This small diamond-shaped medallion belonged to Dr Macklin, who had remained on Elephant Island. It commemorates their rescue by the Chilean naval tug *Yelcho*, in Shackleton's fourth attempt on 30 August 1916.

This time there was no ice as they approached Elephant Island, only fog, through which Shackleton was allowed to close the land at some risk during the night of 29 August, increasingly anxious that wind and current might bring the ice back in. Worsley's navigation was again excellent but they nearly missed Cape Wild by approaching from the unfamiliar western side rather than the east. That was quickly resolved and at 1pm on 30th they were lying off the spit in conditions almost alarmingly calm. Shackleton went off in a boat and found an excited and emotional party all well on shore where they had almost given up hope. He superstitiously refused to land at all and insisted on immediate evacuation.

Wild had long made the party live in a state of readiness to move at short notice. Within an hour everyone was embarked, the remains of the camp and *Endurance*'s last two boats were abandoned and *Yelcho* headed fast for the open sea before its luck could turn. On 3 September 1916 they made a triumphant entry into Punta Arenas, cheered by Chileans and members of the English, German and Austrian communities alike, the war notwithstanding. With his thoughts now turning to how the world would react to his epic of survival snatched from the jaws of failure, and the story to be made of it, Shackleton had of course ensured they did not arrive without advance fanfare.

VOYAGES' END

8

By Jeremy Michell and Pieter van der Merwe

The race to the South Pole in the years before the First World War involved more people, of many nationalities, than have appeared in this brief account of the three names that dominate British perception of it.

Scott, like Nelson, has been assured immortality in the British pantheon by the manner of his death. The fact that it occurred in what was popularly seen as a close-run if unsuccessful contest for a national goal made him a British Imperial hero. Since then, and also like Nelson, the passing of Empire itself has prompted reconsiderations that have inevitably questioned his competence, if not his tragic status.

Historical perspective, of course, makes it easy to criticise Scott. It does him greater justice to recognise that, far more than Amundsen or Shackleton, he was a conventional product of his background – English, Naval, Victorian – and to a degree, a casualty of its limitations as well as any personal factors. Had he been different, as Amundsen was – both as a Norwegian and in cast of mind – and Shackleton too as an unconventional, romantic adventurer, neither Markham nor his committee-men would have backed him. On the scientific front, his expeditions achieved wide and important results but he did not have the outlook, skills or competitive focus by which Amundsen beat him to the Pole, or the natural leadership gifts by which Shackleton achieved more in defeat than his practical failings and improvisations probably deserved.

One aspect of Scott, which should at least be noted, is the question of how far his temperament – introspective, sensitive and with both charm and notable literary gifts – may have been incompatible with the career he chose, or at least with the extreme circumstances into which it led him.

Anton Omelchenko, dwarfed by the enormous size of the Barne Glacier, Antarctica. The sheer scale of the landscape presented challenges for polar photographers, who resorted to placing crew in their photographs to provide a sense of scale. Photograph by Herbert Ponting, December 1911. OPPOSITE

There has been no scope to do more than hint at this here but, if such a contradiction has any substance, it would deepen both the nature of Scott's tragedy and the respect due to the bravery with which he met his death.

That death, however, and the rationalisation of pointless sacrifices in the Great War so soon afterwards, put Scott beyond immediate criticism. Neither Amundsen nor Shackleton were so lucky. Nothing that either did afterwards matched, in the former's case, winning the race to the South Pole and, in the latter's, his escape from it. Both had to live with anticlimax.

Although various delays and the war intervened, Amundsen continued to explore. He built a new ice ship, the *Maud*, in which from July 1918 he began a seven-year attempt to accomplish his drift across the Arctic Ocean. Thanks to the vagaries of wind and current, however, *Maud* only succeeded in traversing its edges, through the North-East Passage (the second ship to do so), and Amundsen did not complete the full voyage himself.

During the war, aged 50, he had learned to fly and, despite personal bankruptcy and other difficulties, he began a series of attempts to cross the North Pole by air in 1923. In 1925 he and his companions were nearly stranded after one of their two planes was damaged in a forced landing on the Arctic pack. The following year, however, Amundsen and the Italian Primo Nobile succeeded in flying over the North Pole from Spitzbergen to Alaska in the Italian-built airship *Norge*. The flight restored Amundsen's flagging reputation and public popularity but he then quarrelled with Nobile and others, and his last years were increasingly isolated and occupied with efforts to clear his debts. He was eventually successful but, unfortunately, the bitter tone of his autobiography did little to help his public image when it appeared in 1927.

In 1928 Nobile made another flight to the Pole in the airship *Italia* but disappeared on the return. As a matter of honour, Amundsen rapidly became involved in the ill-coordinated rescue attempts, his name inducing the French government to provide a Latham flying-boat and crew for

Maud, **named after** the Queen of Norway, was built in 1916 to Amundsen's design to complete a north-polar drift. However, the expedition completed the North-East Passage instead. TOP RIGHT

The flight of the airship *Norge* across the Arctic in 1926 meant that Amundsen and Wisting became the only men to have seen both the North and South Poles to that date. BOTTOM RIGHT

The **seven surviving men** from the Ross Sea party, Andrew Jack, Alexander Stevens, Ritchie Richards, Harry Ernest Wild, Irvine Gaze, Ernest Joyce and John Cope, are pictured along with (at far right) Shackleton and Captain John King Davis of the *Aurora*. The whole group suffered enormous privations when *Aurora* broke loose in a gale. However, their successful completion of depot laying for Shackleton reflected their determination not to fail. ABOVE

Shackleton (shown right on board *Quest*) was no longer well by the time of the *Quest* project but his sudden death on 5 January 1922 was a shock. Frank Wild, who had accompanied him on every Antarctic expedition, called it 'a staggering blow'. RIGHT

the purpose. With his pilot companion Leif Dietrichson and the French crew of four under Captain René Guilbaud, Amundsen took off from Tromsø on 18 June 1928. They were never seen again. Wreckage found in the sea months later suggested they had made a forced landing and subsequently perished in circumstances that can only be imagined. For Amundsen it was a tragic but perhaps fitting end. Nobile was rescued by others.

Shackleton and his crew were welcomed as heroes in South America in 1916. They finally parted at Buenos Aires and Shackleton made his way to join *Aurora* in New Zealand for the rescue of the Ross Sea party. They returned to Wellington on 9 February 1917, again to a considerable welcome. Shackleton's return to England in May, after lecturing in America, was notably quiet by comparison. He was already actively seeking a role in the war, aware of a degree of criticism for being so long absent from it; 'messing about on icebergs', in one reported phrase.

Initially he was unsuccessful, but between October 1917 and the spring of 1918 he was sent on a British propaganda mission to South America. In July 1918, after his return, Shackleton was gazetted temporary major in the army and became involved in a semi-commercial expedition to establish a British presence in Spitsbergen, in which Wild and McIlroy were also employed (the latter now invalided from the army through wounds suffered at Ypres). In August at Tromsø, however, he was taken ill with what McIlroy thought was a heart attack but, as usual, he resisted investigation.

From there he was suddenly called home to organise transport aspects of a new military mission to Murmansk. This outlasted the end of the war, becoming ongoing British support for the regional government against the Bolshevik threat. Shackleton extended it into proposing schemes for local economic development, which, had they worked out, would have provided him with a post-war future. Unsurprisingly, his return to England in March 1919 and the withdrawal of British forces later that year saw the whole effort collapse and the area fell to the communists.

His peacetime life again became a search for income, initially by a drudging round of lecturing on the *Endurance* expedition, from December 1919 to May

1920. As we have seen, this included providing a live commentary to Hurley's remarkable silent film, *In the Grip of the Polar Ice*, twice a day at the Philharmonic Hall. Shackleton's book of the expedition, *South* (again ghosted by Edward Saunders) appeared to a good reception in December 1919. Shackleton gained nothing by it, having assigned the royalties to the heirs of one of his more unforgiving creditors, and he was never to clear many of his other *Endurance* debts. By this time his marriage was also one of form rather than substance and he was spending an increasingly rootless existence with his mistress, Rosalind Chetwynd, or otherwise on the move. He was also drinking and smoking too much, and visibly ageing.

The crew of the *Quest* included a number who had served with Shackleton in the Antarctic before. The ship was not really suitable for the conditions, limiting the expedition's ability to fulfil its aims.

Early in 1920 he began to say he wanted to see the polar regions again, forming plans for the Canadian Arctic for which he was offered backing by a wealthy former school friend, John Quiller Rowett. When Canadian support proved elusive, Rowett generously agreed to a vague alternative plan to circumnavigate Antarctica and fix the position of various ill-charted islands. In three months, Shackleton put together his last expedition in the 125-ton sealer *Quest*. For this he surrounded himself with old friends, a number of whom were still owed money from *Endurance* days: Wild, Worsley, Macklin, McIlroy and Hussey were among them, and new faces too. They sailed from London on 21 September 1921, via Plymouth, Madeira and Rio de Janeiro. Shackleton was now clearly in poor health, increasingly listless, nostalgic and a cause of concern to the doctors. At Rio he had a heart attack but again refused to be properly examined.

On 4 January 1922, a fine day turned into a wonderful evening, and they were welcomed at Grytviken in South Georgia by old Norwegian friends. Shackleton had already confessed that he had no clear plans thereafter and McIlroy later recalled that, on leaving Plymouth, the tolling of a bell-buoy had prompted him to remark, 'That's my death knell'. On board *Quest* in the small hours of the following morning, 5 January, Macklin came to his urgent call and found him

Shackleton's cabin on board *Quest*. James Marr, a boy scout on the expedition, wrote of it as his 'sea-bedroom' and said it 'was little better than a glorified packing-case; it measured seven feet by six...'.

in the middle of another heart attack. As he had often done before, the doctor told him he would have to change his ways. '"You're always wanting me to give up things," said Shackleton, "what is it you want me to give up?" I replied "Chiefly alcohol, Boss, I don't think it agrees with you."'

It was their last exchange: Shackleton died within minutes, three weeks short of his 48th birthday. With Hussey as escort, his body was sent home for burial but only got as far as Montevideo. There a message was received from Emily, always the forgiving and understanding wife, that her ever-restless husband should remain where his heart lay, in the Southern Ocean. On 5 March 1922, the remote way-station of all his voyages became his final harbour when he was buried on South Georgia, in the Norwegian whalers' cemetery at Grytviken.

Legacies

The legacies of Scott, Shackleton and Amundsen are still evident today. Interest in the men continues as biographies analyse their personalities, decisions, skills and successes. Over time the reputations of all three have waxed and waned, with some surviving criticism better than others and a few biographers having to rescue reputations. For example, Sir Ranulph Fiennes's 2003 life of Scott was in response to his own experiences and Roland Huntford's comparative biography of Scott and Amundsen from 1979, which was controversially harsh on the former. Shackleton's reputation was long overshadowed by Scott's but in recent years he has been used to illustrate leadership skills, especially in adversity. At the National Maritime Museum, Shackleton was one of a number of historical figures in the 'Leading Lives' educational programme supporting A-Level Business Studies courses. This used his Antarctic leadership style and actions to analyse leadership characteristics for a modern audience. A more recent biography of Amundsen, always a difficult character for the British, casts him in a more complicated light than just an unsporting adventurer who stole Scott's crown by reaching the South Pole first.

The public perception of Scott and Shackleton, partly informed by such biographies, is neatly summed up in the BBC's 2002 programme *100 Greatest Britons*, in which Shackleton came one ahead of Captain James Cook at 11th, and Scott, one behind Lawrence of Arabia, was 54th. These characters have inspired films like *Scott of the Antarctic* (1948) with John Mills in the title role, and TV programmes such as Channel 4's *Shackleton* (2002), recreating the 1914 *Endurance* expedition and *James Caird* boat journey. The use of their own words added to the feel of authenticity and anticipation, giving viewers an opportunity to see into their world. These films and programmes build on the contemporary filming by Ponting and Hurley. When modern expeditions to the South Pole have been broadcast, the audience gets a sense of the stresses that explorers endure in mind and body. The 2013 'Walking with the Wounded South Pole Allied Challenge' saw 21 servicemen with physical or cognitive injuries travel to the Pole with Prince Harry. The expedition members had to deal with extreme conditions as well as their own disabilities. The Antarctic is also becoming more familiar as a result of the increasing number of visually spectacular wildlife programmes on television, which open up the continent like never before. Equally important are the vast number of images and amount of information about Antarctica that can be accessed on the Internet.

Shackleton's grave in the whaling cemetery on South Georgia. He was buried here at the request of Lady Shackleton, surrounded by the bleak wilderness that played a part in his fame.

Shackleton's love of poetry was reflected in this epitaph. He paraphrased both AC Swinburne and Robert Browning to pay tribute to Macintosh, Spencer-Smith and Hayward, members of the Ross Sea depot-laying party for the *Endurance* expedition.

The recent anniversaries of the *Terra Nova* and *Fram* expeditions (1910/2010) and the more recent Imperial Trans-Antarctic Expedition with the 'Shackleton 100' commemorations (1914/2014) have again raised people's awareness of the men, their stories and their fellow Antarctic veterans. These events are usually linked with concerted efforts to tell the story through public displays. For instance, the redesigned Oates Gallery at the Gilbert White House, Selborne, opened in 2012 as part of the centenary commemorations of Scott's polar attempt; and the Royal Geo-graphical Society's exhibition *The Enduring Eye* in 2015 used the excetional artistic photography of Frank Hurley to retell the story of the *Endurance* expedition of 1914–1916 for a new audience. These anniversaries are occasions to focus on acquiring new material to support the personal stories from the polar expeditions. The Scott Polar Research Institute successfully received funding to acquire prints and, later, the negatives taken by Captain Scott during his last expedition. These show life on the journey south from his perspective.

While much research has focused on the leaders, biographers are now beginning to focus on the scientists, sailors and adventurers who followed and supported them. These men were also willing to put their own lives at risk for a variety of complicated, and at times personal, reasons. To give a more rounded view of the early years of Antarctic exploration, there is still room for further research on the expedition crews and their experiences. These men, individually sometimes described as either a 'Scott man' or a 'Shackleton man', were not only often inspired by their leaders, but their exploits have also inspired others to read about them and even visit the Antarctic, to try to understand what the appeal was, or to experience the harshness of the environment first-hand.

Tourism to Antarctica, mainly through specialist cruises, has increased in the last 15 years from 17,543 people (the combined total for those that landed or stayed on board ship) in 2002–2003 to 37,405 in 2013–2014. The peak for this period was in the Antarctic summer of 2007–2008 when 46,069 visited the Antarctic region, of which 33,054 landed on the islands or the continent.[1] By contrast, 100 years before, in 1907–1908, only 15 men lived at Cape Royds during Shackleton's 1907 British Antarctic Expedition. This increased tourism has implications that need careful management in order to reduce its environmental impact and preserve the huts, landscape and seas.

Many of the utilitarian early Antarctic research stations' exploration huts, and other things these expeditions left there have now been actively conserved or are under restoration, reflecting their modern status as historic, commemorative buildings. The work includes preserving their varied contents, which range from paper and fabrics to evocatively branded packaging, tinned foodstuffs and equipment. A number of these huts and stations are in the care of the Cambridge-based UK Antarctic Heritage Trust (established in 1993), whose 'flagship' base for summer visitation is Port Lockroy. This is a former base built in 1944 during Operation Tabarin, a secret mission during the Second World War to establish a permanent British presence in the Antarctic. The Scott and Shackleton huts discussed in this book are now in the hands of the New Zealand Antarctic Heritage Trust, founded in 1987. Both Trusts aim to preserve and promote these structures to help future generations understand and appreciate the Antarctic, and the stories of its exploration that they embody. Luckily for those who wish to remain 'armchair' polar explorers, Shackleton's and Scott's expedition huts (1907–1909 and 1911–1913 respectively) have been extensively photographed, so that visitors can view them online and imagine themselves living there during the 'Heroic Age'.

In a role reversal from the polar expeditions where staged photographs of expedition members with sponsored foodstuffs were obligatory, Scott and Shackleton

---

1   http://www.coolantarctica.com/Antarctica%20fact%20file/science/threats_tourism.php
     Retrieved, 3 March 2017

are now brands in their own right. 'Captain Scott Tea', as originally blended for his 1910 expedition, is available, as is Shackleton-branded clothing, inspired by that taken on his expeditions or worn by him. Similarly, three bottles of Mackinley's whisky were removed from a case found during the restoration work on Shackleton's 1907 hut at Cape Royds. The blend was analysed and has since been recreated for a modern market as 'Mackinley's Shackleton Rare Old Highland Malt'. Even Amundsen does not escape. His name is associated with skincare products and outdoor clothing that link back to his successes as an explorer.

In many ways, it was science that sold these expeditions to the various establishments, institutions and funders, even if science was not the primary focus. Scott was certainly scientifically minded with a curiosity to find out more about the Antarctic. Shackleton recognised that he needed scientists on his expeditions as a way of legitimising his desire to seek 'firsts'. Similarly, when writing about his expedition to the South Pole, Amundsen stated that 'on this little detour, science would have to look after itself' as he was focused on attaining the Pole. This is a bit unfair as it ignores the valuable work undertaken by the *Fram* after the shore party had been dropped off at the Bay of Whales, and the meteorological records kept by the men who remained at the Antarctic base of Framheim, on the Ross Sea ice edge.

All three British expeditions generated a large amount of scientific research, much of which was published over a number of years. This includes more than 50 scientific reports from the *Discovery* expedition alone, while Shackleton's 1907 expedition scientists published their findings in a wide range of journals between 1910 and 1914. The body of work created by these expeditions, now available to future scientists working in the Antarctic, acts as a starting point to understanding the changes in its climate and landscape. An interesting by-product of this research is in understanding how weather conditions may have affected Scott's returning party. The meteorological and temperature readings gathered by scientists such as George Simpson, and the numerous sledging parties, have been compared with the automated results received between 1986 and 1999. Susan Solomon's analysis of Scott's last expedition uses these records to highlight how the extraordinary weather and temperature patterns in March 1912 had a negative impact on the Polar Party on its return march.

The logbooks from the various British expedition ships, as well as those from French, Belgian and German expeditions, have been used to analyse the extent of summer sea ice around Antarctica between 1897 and 1917. This has been compared to satellite information from 1989 to 2014. The results have allowed scientists to improve mapping of the variations in the summer sea-ice limits over a longer period and to try to understand the impact of climate change on the Antarctic.[2] On a more personal level, Tim Jarvis used his 2013 recreation of Shackleton's boat journey and crossing of South Georgia to highlight the climatic changes in the last 100 years. South Georgia's glaciers have retreated 97 per cent since 1916, resulting in Jarvis's team crossing a heavily crevassed glacier rather than a vast snowscape that Shackleton would have recognised. More worryingly, the König Glacier had retreated so far that the team found an Alpine meadow in its place.

Many institutions have these early expeditions to thank for setting a scientific agenda in the Antarctic. In the UK, there is the British Antarctic Survey (BAS), which can trace its history back to Operation Tabarin, the Second World War mission mentioned on page 183. However, BAS's spiritual history starts with the science undertaken by the early polar scientists. After the war, Tabarin transformed into the Falkland Islands Dependencies Survey and broadened its remit into science and exploration before becoming the BAS in 1962. Its continuing focus on collaborative international research is a legacy of which pre-First World War pioneers would have been proud.

An institution with direct links to the expeditions led by Scott and Shackleton is the Scott Polar Research Institute. It was established in 1920 as a memorial to Captain Scott and his companions, with the aim of undertaking research in nat-

---

2   http://www.the-cryosphere.net/10/2721/2016/tc-10-2721-2016.pdf   Estimating the extent of Antarctic summer sea ice during the Heroic Age of Antarctic Exploration, retrieved 27 February 2017

ural and social sciences that relate to the polar regions. The first director was Frank Debenham, the geologist on the 1910 expedition. He was supported by Raymond Priestley, another geologist who accompanied him in 1910, and James Wordie, the geologist and chief scientist from Shackleton's 1914 expedition. In turn, James Wordie was very supportive of the 1955–1958 Commonwealth Trans-Antarctic Expedition, which achieved the 1914 goal that he attempted with Shackleton. An important scientific legacy these expeditions left was the number of scientists with Antarctic experience and understanding, who were able to support and encourage the next generation well into the second half of the 20th century.

The significance of the Antarctic as a place of science was confirmed by the 18-month research programme undertaken during the International Geophysical Year (IGY), 1957–1958. The success of the IGY resulted in the Antarctic Treaty of 1959, which came into force in 1961 and overcame the more politically confrontational nature of superpower relations at the time. This treaty confirmed that 'Antarctica shall continue for ever to be used exclusively for peaceful purposes and shall not become the scene or object of international discord', and defined Antarctica as anything below 60° south. It also banned military activity, such as establishing bases or fortifications, and nuclear testing and disposal. Importantly, the treaty promoted a spirit of international scientific cooperation between the signatories through sharing results and personnel. In order to make this a success, participants had to agree to a 'freeze' on claims of territorial sovereignty, especially where they overlapped. It also prevents further claims on the continent until the treaty expires. There are now 53 signatories in differing membership categories, up from the original 12 that signed in 1959. Other treaties are linked to the Antarctic Treaty creating the Antarctic Treaty System to ensure that the continent remains 'a natural reserve, devoted to peace and science'. There are currently nearly 80 research stations there, of which around 40 are all-year-round bases, and are run (in some cases on a shared basis) by 31 different countries.

The scientific programme of the IGY included overland expeditions with echoes of those led by Amundsen, Scott and Shackleton. The most significant and well-reported, not least on newsreel film and television, was the highly mecha-nised Commonwealth Trans-Antarctic Expedition (1955–1958) led by Dr Vivian Fuchs and Sir Edmund Hillary, which first crossed the continent via the South Pole, just over half a century on from Shackleton's attempt. Fuchs's party of 12 men left their temporary 'Shackleton Base' on the Weddell ice edge in November 1957 and covered the 3,508km (2,180 miles) to the newly built New Zealand Scott Base, near Scott's original 1902 hut on Ross Island, McMurdo Sound, in 99 days. Hillary's team had, in the meantime, laid depots south from McMurdo towards the Pole, reaching it on 3 January 1958. Hillary's arrival at the Pole was not orig-inally planned but he pushed on there, making his group the first to reach it overland since Scott. The first Americans only arrived by air in 1956, prior to constructing their Amundsen–Scott Base at the Pole in preparation for the IGY. This base, today greatly developed in terms of the scientific work done there, was built from materials airlifted in from the US McMurdo Station on Ross Island, also built for the IGY close to Scott's original 1902 hut.

The IGY spurred on other expeditions with combined science and 'first-attainment' goals. The Russian 1957–1958 overland expeditions reached both the (then) South Geomagnetic Pole and the Pole of Relative Inaccessibility (the fur-thest point inland from the sea) at 3,658 metres (12,000 feet) up and 2,012km (1,250 miles) inland. They undertook scientific work and the mapping of uncharted areas of the continent as they went. Since then at least ten parties have crossed the continent. For example, in 1980–1981 Sir Ranulph Fiennes led a three-man party in his British Transglobe Expedition, using sledge-pulling skidoos and fol-lowing the 0/180° meridian, which took them 67 days. As if that was not enough, he returned with Dr Mike Stroud in 1992 to complete the first totally unsupported crossing via the Pole, completing 2,170km (1,350 miles) in 95 days. Will Steger, with an international team of six men, undertook the longest overland expedition in 1989–1990, from the tip of the Antarctic Peninsula via the South Pole to the Russian Mirny Base on the eastern coast – a distance of some 5,955km (3,700 miles) that took seven months. By comparison to the length of all such continen-tal transits, Amundsen's high-speed dash from the Ross Sea up the Axel Heiberg

Glacier, which won the race to the Pole, was about 1,300km/810 miles (700 nautical miles). Scott's tragic, trudging march to it up the Beardmore, the *via dolorosa* of Antarctic discovery as one writer has called it, was 1,416km/880 miles (about 760 nautical miles).

In more recent times, the nature of overland expeditions has evolved with a greater emphasis on attaining 'firsts' of a more personal nature, such as method of transport, the course taken and personnel, rather than being for scientific purposes only. Journeys have become 'self-discovery' challenges for those making them, or undertaken in support of charitable causes, which helps underpin their costs through sponsorship. To take a few examples: in 1989, despite women having worked as part of the Antarctic scientific community for decades, the American Victoria Murden was the first to reach the Pole by land on skis. The first man to cycle there on a route of 1,247km (775 miles) was Daniel Burton in 2013–2014, while the youngest (so far) to complete the journey from the coast is Lewis Clarke, who was 16 years and 61 days old when he arrived at the Pole on 18 January 2014. A small group of people are motivated by their family links to Antarctica, such as Patrick Bergel, Shackleton's great-grandson. Bergel completed the first crossing of Antarctica in a passenger car using a modified Hyundai Santa Fe in early 2017 to commemorate Shackleton's attempt in 1914–1917. In a similar vein, Alice Holmes, the granddaughter of Sir James Wordie, walked and skied the final 160km (100 miles) to the South Pole with her husband and David Hempleman-Adams in December 2015. She was motivated by a feeling of 'unfinished business' and a wish to create a legacy by raising money to digitise Wordie's diaries and other relevant papers from the 1914 Imperial Trans-Antarctic Expedition. It has to be noted, however, that many such 'challenge' journeys to the Pole are one-way, with the return being by air.

These modern expeditions are also very different in other ways to those undertaken by Scott, Shackleton and Amundsen, for whom there was no continental support structure and, for the British parties, little training in advance of arriving on the continent. While expeditions are still high-risk, modern communications mean that relevant authorities can be alerted quickly and rescue by air can be within days during the Antarctic summer. Additionally, a number have support teams to provide immediate assistance. This, however, is not the case in the winter months, when scientists left at the research stations know they are almost on their own. Ron Shemenski, a physicist who was rescued during the Antarctic winter in 2001, described the Amundsen–Scott station at the South Pole during winter as 'a place that's harder to get to than the International Space Station'.

Whatever the time of year, the early explorers had to be more self-reliant and deal with situations as they arose in isolation from the outside world. Shackleton, for example, had to save himself after *Endurance* sank in 1915. The time that the British government then required to equip and send a relief ship south to pick up his men from Elephant Island was longer than he needed (including three failed attempts) to effect their rescue himself from South America. Today, increased contact with the continent also means there is little need to overwinter in Antarctica before undertaking an expedition. This reduces the logistical challenges and the costs involved. The clothing and equipment has undergone refinement and new technology has helped to make it lighter and more efficient, although some still prefer old ways for practical reasons, such as string ties instead of zips as they are easier to repair. This does not take anything away from the endeavours of people who nowadays attempt to conquer some aspect of Antarctica, but highlights the different challenges they face and how extraordinary the achievements of the early expeditions were, more than 100 years ago.

While the scientific community has a permanent presence on the Antarctic continent, most other human activity is transient and seasonal. The high interior remains vast, bleak and largely empty, but while still *terra deserta* it is no longer *terra incognita*. The 'Heroic-Age' explorers and scientists blazed trails there that others of many nations have followed, multiplied and greatly broadened in the last century, and continue to do so. History and landscape aside, Antarctica's critical climatic significance for the environmental stability of the world, and the research work undertaken there in many fields from Earth sciences to medicine and astronomy, keep it well in the public eye.

CREW LISTS

Key personnel

DISCOVERY 1901–1904

Officers and Scientists

Robert Falcon Scott, Captain RN *leader*

Albert B Armitage, (first) Lieutenant, RNR *navigator and second-in-command*

Michael Barne, Lieutenant, RN *magnetician*

Louis C Bernacchi *physicist*

Hartley T Ferrar *geologist*

Thomas V Hodgson *marine biologist*

Reginald Koettlitz *surgeon*

George FA Mulock, (second) Lieutenant, RN

Charles Royds, Lieutenant, RN *meteorologist*

Ernest H Shackleton, Sub-Lieutenant RNR, (and third lieutenant),* *surveyor and photographer*

Reginald Skelton, Lieutenant (E) RN, Chief Engineer*

Edward A Wilson *assistant surgeon, artist and zoologist*

Warrant Officers (all RN)

Thomas A Feather, Boatswain

James H Dellbridge, Second Engineer

Frederick E Dailet *carpenter*

Charles F Ford *steward*

Petty Officers (all RN)

Jacob Cross, PO

Edgar Evans, PO

William Smythe, PO

David Allan, PO

Thomas Kennar, PO

William MacFarlane, PO*

Seamen

Arthur Pilbeam, RN

William L Heald, RN

James Dell, RN

Frank Wild, RN

Thomas Williamson, RN

George Croucher, RN

Ernest Joyce, RN

Thomas Crean, RN

Jesse Handsley, RN

William J Weller, MN *dog handler*

William Peters, RN*

John Walker, MN*

James Duncan, MN* *shipwright*

George Vince, RN (died March 1902)

Charles Bonner, RN (died December 1901)

Stokers

William Lashly, RN

Arthur L Quartley, RN

Thomas Whitfield, RN

Frank Plumley, RN

William Page, RN*

William Hubert, MN*

Royal Marines

Arthur Blissett, lance corporal

Gilbert Scott, private

Civilians

Henry Brett* *cook*

Charles Clarke *cook*

Clarence Hare* *assistant steward*

Horace Buckbridge* *laboratory assistant*

NIMROD 1907–1909

Ernest H Shackleton *leader*

TW Edgeworth David *chief scientist*

Jameson Boyd-Adams *meteorologist*

Philip Brocklehurst *assistant geologist and surveyor*

Bernard Day *motor specialist*

Ernest Joyce *in charge of dogs, sledges and equipment*

Alistair Mackay *surgeon and biologist*

Douglas Mawson *physicist*

Bertram Armytage *in charge of ponies*

Eric Marshall *surgeon and cartographer*

George Marston *artist*

George Murray-Levick *biologist*

Raymond Priestley *geologist*

William Cook *cook*

Frank Wild *in charge of stores*

* The list is taken from Scott's *Voyage of the 'Discovery'*; added to it are the men who spent only one Antarctic winter with the expedition, marked with an asterisk, who – with the exception of Shackleton and Mulock – were not listed in the book. Clarke took over duties of cook from Brett. Scott ran *Discovery* on naval lines but, with an entirely volunteer crew including civilians, as a merchant vessel in legal terms.

TERRA NOVA 1910–1913

Robert Falcon Scott, Captain, CVO, RN *leader*

George P Abbot, PO, RN

WW Archer, late RN, *chief steward*

Edward L Atkinson, RN, *surgeon and parasitologist*

Henry R Bowers, Lieutenant, Royal Indian Marine

Frank V Browning, PO, 2nd class RN

Wilfrid M Bruce, Lieutenant, RN

Victor LA Campbell, Lieutenant, RN

Thomas Clissold, late RN *cook*

Thomas Crean, PO, RN

Apsley Cherry-Garrard *assistant zoologist*

Bernard C Day *motor specialist*

Frank Debenham *geologist*

Henry Dickason, AB, RN

Francis RH Drake, Assistant Paymaster, RN

Edgar Evans, PO, RN

Edward RGR Evans, Lieutenant, RN

Robert Forde, PO, RN

Dimitri Gerov *dog driver*

Tryggve Gran, Sub-Lieutenant, Norwegian *ski expert*

FJ Hooper, late RN *steward*

W Lashly, *chief stoker*

G Murray Levick, RN, *surgeon*

Dennis G Lillie *biologist*

Cecil H Meares *in charge of dog teams*

Lawrence EG Oates, Captain, 6th Inniskilling Dragoons

Anton Omelchenko *groom*

Harry LL Pennell, Lieutenant, RN

Herbert G Ponting *camera artist*

Raymond E Priestley *geologist*

Edward W Nelson *biologist*

Henry F de P Rennick, Lieutenant, RN

George C Simpson *meteorologist*

T Griffith Taylor *geologist*

Thomas S Williamson, PO, RN

Edward A Wilson *chief of the scientific staff and zoologist*

Charles S Wright *physicist*

ENDURANCE 1914–1916

Ernest H Shackleton *leader*

William Bakewell, *seaman*

Percy Blackborrow *stowaway – later steward*

Alfred Cheetham, Third Officer

Robert Clark *biologist*

Thomas Crean, Second Officer

Charles Green *cook*

Lionel Greenstreet, First Officer

Ernest Holness *fireman*

Walter How, *seaman*

Hubert Hudson, Second Officer

Frank Hurley *camera artist*

Leonard Hussey *meteorologist*

Reginald James *physicist*

Alfred Kerr, Second Engineer

Timothy McCarthy, *seaman*

James McIlroy *surgeon*

Thomas McLeod, *seaman*

Henry McNeish *carpenter*

Alexander Macklin, *chief surgeon*

George Marston *artist*

Thomas Orde-Lees (Lieutenant, RM) *ski expert and store keeper*

Louis Rickinson, Chief Engineer

William Stephenson, *stoker*

John Vincent, Boatswain

Frank Wild, Second-in-Command

James Wordie *geologist*

Frank Worsley, Master and navigator

SELECTED BIOGRAPHIES

Amundsen, Roald Englebreth Graving (1872–1928)
See Chapter 4 (page 78) and 8 (page 174)

Armitage, Albert (1864–1943) Armitage was a cadet in HMS *Worcester* before joining the P&O line in 1886. In 1894 he was released to serve as navigator on the Jackson–Harmsworth expedition to Franz Josef Land in the Arctic where he remained for two and a half years. He returned to P&O in 1896, before being appointed navigator and second-in-command on the *Discovery* expedition in May 1900.

Atkinson, Edward Leicester (1882–1929) After qualifying in 1906 at St Thomas's Hospital Medical School, Atkinson went on to serve at the Royal Naval Hospital, Haslar. He joined the *Terra Nova* expedition in 1910 as junior surgeon and parasitologist and led the search party that discovered Scott's body in November 1912. He was awarded the Albert Medal during the First World War and had to retire from the Royal Navy at the age of 46 due to injuries sustained in it.

Barne, Michael (1887–1961) Michael Barne joined the Navy in 1893. He served as second lieutenant on the *Discovery* expedition. Barne attempted to organise his own expedition to the Weddell Sea after the *Discovery*, but had to abandon the idea when he failed to raise sufficient funds. Frostbite injuries to his hands prevented him from serving on the *T erra Nova* expedition.

Bernacchi, Louis (1876–1942) A Tasmanian, Bernacchi had been one of the men to winter at Cape Adare as part of the *Southern Cross* expedition in 1899. He joined the *Discovery* expedition as physicist and was responsible for seismic and magnetic research. His own colourful account, *Saga of the 'Discovery'*, was published in 1938.

Borchgrevink, Carsten Egeberg (1864–1934)
Borchgrevink was a Norwegian and childhood friend of Roald Amundsen. He travelled to Australia in 1888 and, after a variety of jobs, signed on as a crew member in the *Antarctic*, a Norwegian sealer, in 1894. When a party landed at Cape Adare in 1895, during its voyage, Borchgrevink was one of the first men to set foot on Antarctica. Inspired by his experience and determined to be the first man to winter on the continent, by 1899 Borchgrevink had raised sufficient funds from a British sponsor, Sir George Newnes, to return as leader of his own expedition in the *Southern Cross*. He successfully spent the winter of 1899–1900 at Cape Adare and travelled south by sledge to latitude 78° 50' – at that time, the furthest south ever reached.

Bowers, Henry Robertson, (called 'Birdie', 1883–1912)
Bowers was descended from a Scottish seafaring family. He earned the nickname 'Birdie' from his distinctive nose. In September 1897 he was enrolled as a cadet in HMS *Worcester* from where he entered the merchant service. In 1905 he left to join the Royal Indian Marine as a sub-lieutenant. He had read Scott's account of the *Discovery* expedition and had a lifetime fascination with polar exploration. He was recommended for the *Terra Nova* expedition by Sir Clements Markham and approved by his former commander in HMS *Worcester*. He died with Scott and Wilson on their return journey from the Pole.

Bruce, Wilfred Montagu (1874–1953) Kathleen Scott's brother, Wilfred Bruce had served as a cadet in HMS *Worcester* before joining the merchant navy. He joined the *Terra Nova* expedition, supporting Meares in transporting dogs and ponies selected for the expedition from Vladivostok to New Zealand.

Campbell, Victor Lindsey Arbuthnot (1875–1956)
Victor Campbell served on the *Terra Nova* expedition
where he was picked by Scott to lead what became the
Eastern Party – later known as the Northern Party when
they were put ashore at Cape Adare – the area originally
explored by Borchgrevink. Known as 'the Mate' or the
'Wicked Mate', Campbell and his five companions spent
seven months of the 1912 winter in a 2.7 x 1.5-metre
(9x5-foot) ice cave, cut off from relief and lacking
adequate equipment and rations. They then sledged
the 200-mile journey back to Cape Evans, only to learn
that Scott and his four companions had died nine
months earlier.

Cherry-Garrard, Apsley George Benet (1886–1959)
Selected by Wilson to join the scientific team on the
Terra Nova expedition as assistant zoologist, 'Cherry',
as he was known, travelled with Wilson and Bowers on
their extraordinary winter journey to collect Emperor
penguin eggs in 1911. His own fine account of the *Terra
Nova* expedition, *The Worst Journey in the World*, was
published in 1922. In it he showed his misgivings that
had he disobeyed his orders and travelled on beyond
One Ton depot to look for Scott's return sledging party,
they might have been saved.

Colbeck, Lt William Robinson (1871–1930) Colbeck
was a Yorkshireman who sailed with Borchgrevink to
Antarctica in 1898, one of only three British subjects
on this largely Scandinavian-manned British Antarctic
Expedition. He was one of those who reached
Borchgrevink's 'furthest south' with him. He was also
captain of the *Morning*, the relief ship sent to effect
the release and rescue of the ice-bound *Discovery* in
1902–03 and again in 1903–04.

Crean, Thomas (1876–1938) Crean was born at
Annascaul in County Kerry, Ireland. He joined the
Discovery as an able seaman and his powerful build
marked him as an excellent sledger. He went on to serve
on the *Terra Nova* expedition from HMS *Bulwark* and
was awarded the Albert Medal for saving the life of
Teddy Evans. Crean then bought himself out of the
Navy in 1912 in order to join Shackleton's *Endurance*
expedition, during which he was one of the six who
sailed to South Georgia in the *James Caird* and then
crossed the mountainous island on foot with Shackleton
and Worsley to find help at Stromness. He later returned
to Annascaul to open a pub called 'The South Pole Inn'.
A man of extraordinary physical and mental toughness,
Crean eventually died of appendicitis.

David, Sir TW Edgeworth (1858–1934) Although
Welsh-born and Oxford-educated, David's career is
linked with Australia, where he became a geological
surveyor in 1882 and Professor of Geology at Sydney
University in 1891. He was particularly interested in
past geological climates and was elected a Fellow of
the Royal Society in 1900. After giving Shackleton
much help with the *Nimrod* expedition he was invited
to join it as chief scientist. He led the first ascent of
Mount Erebus and it was his party that first located
the South Magnetic Pole. He later rose to the rank of
lieutenant colonel as a military tunnelling expert in
the First World War and was knighted in 1920,
remaining a major figure in his scientific field
throughout the Commonwealth until his sudden
death in 1934.

Debenham, Frank (1883–1959) Born in New South Wales, Debenham was selected by Wilson as a geologist for the *Terra Nova* expedition. 'Deb', as he was known, went on to found the Scott Polar Research Institute in 1920 with James Wordie and Raymond Priestley, becoming its first Director.

Evans, Edgar (1876–1912) Born at Middleton in South Wales, 'Taff' Evans joined the Royal Navy in 1891. He was selected for the *Discovery* expedition and went on to become a physical training officer and naval gunnery instructor in 1904 before volunteering for the *Terra Nova* expedition. He died on the Beardmore Glacier on 17 February 1912, the first casualty of Scott's five-man Polar Party.

Evans, Edward RGR (1881–1957) 'Teddy' Evans joined the Royal Navy from the training ship HMS *Worcester* in 1896. In 1902 he convinced Sir Clements Markham that he should be appointed as second officer in the relief ship *Morning*, which found the *Discovery* in McMurdo Sound. In 1910 he decided to form his own expedition to the South Pole but on hearing of Scott's plans, he offered his services and joined the *Terra Nova* as second-in-command. He was instrumental in gathering support and funds for the expedition. He almost died from scurvy on the Ross Ice Shelf, but was saved by the actions of petty officers Crean and Lashly. He was to return to the Navy after the expedition to become a war hero in command of the destroyer *Broke* and was created a Labour peer in 1946 as Admiral Lord Mountevans.

Ferrar, Hartley T (1879–1932) Hartley Ferrar replaced Dr JW Gregory, who had resigned, as geologist on the *Discovery* expedition. He discovered fossilised remains of early flora in Victoria Land.

Gerov, Dimitri (1888?–1932) Born in eastern Siberia, Gerov (the English spelling of whose name varies considerably) supported Meares in selecting and then transporting the dogs purchased for the *Terra Nova* expedition from Russia to New Zealand and onward to the Antarctic. He joined the expedition as dog handler.

Gran, Tryggve (1889–1980) Introduced to Scott by Fridtjof Nansen, Gran had planned his own expedition but was selected for the *Terra Nova* expedition because of his skiing expertise. He was a member of the search party that discovered Scott's tent. Later, Shackleton failed to persuade him to go on the *Endurance* expedition.

Hodgson, Thomas Vere (1864–1926) In an interlude from his work as Director of the Marine Biological Association Laboratory in Plymouth, Hodgson joined the *Terra Nova* expedition as a biologist, being one of the two eldest members of the party.

Hussey, Leonard (1894–1965) Hussey was meteorologist on the 1914 *Endurance* expedition. He was also a talented musician and entertained the men stranded on Elephant Island with songs and banjo playing.

Hurley, Frank (1886–1962) Frank Hurley bought his first camera at the age of 17. He showed particular talent for landscape photography and set up a postcard business to exploit his skills. In 1910 he was asked by fellow Australian Douglas Mawson to accompany his Australasian Antarctic Expedition of 1911–1914 in the *Aurora*. Hurley created a remarkable range of images and also made the film *Home of the Blizzard*, the documentary that records the expedition. This was seen by Shackleton, who then hired Hurley to join the

Endurance expedition in 1914. As stills and cine-cameraman, Hurley displayed great tenacity and determination while his ingenuity and early training as a metalworker were also enormously useful. He returned to South Georgia in 1916 to shoot additional footage for his film, *South*, which was released in 1919.

James, Reginald (1891–1964) James joined the scientific team on the *Endurance* expedition as a physicist.

Koettlitz, Reginald (1861–1916) Koettlitz had volunteered to serve in the position of doctor on the Jackson–Harmsworth expedition to the Arctic in 1894. He received his appointment as senior surgeon and bacteriologist on the *Discovery* expedition in 1900. A rather serious figure, and the oldest member of the party, his companions gave him the nickname 'Cutlets'.

Lashly, William (1868–1940) Born in Hampshire, Lashly served as leading stoker in the *Discovery*. His strength and dependable nature made him a natural success on the expedition. He went on to serve as an instructor at the Royal Naval College, Osborne, before volunteering for the *Terra Nova* expedition. With Tom Crean, he was awarded the Albert Medal for saving the life of Teddy Evans.

Lillie, Dennis G (1884–1963) Lillie was biologist on the *Terra Nova* expedition.

Markham, Sir Clements (1830–1916) While in the Navy, Markham served on the 1850–1851 expedition to search for the Arctic explorer Sir John Franklin, and went to Greenland on the Nares polar voyage of 1875. He was president of the Royal Geographical Society, 1893–1905, and a passionate advocate of Antarctic exploration, securing Scott's selection as leader for the 1901 *Discovery* expedition.

Marston, George (1882–1940) Born in Southsea, Marston had trained to be an art teacher in London. He joined Shackleton's *Nimrod* and *Endurance* expeditions as artist, recording events that would then illustrate the official accounts of the expeditions. After the *Endurance* expedition he went on to join the Rural Industries Board, of which he was Director from 1934 to his death in 1940.

Mawson, Sir Douglas (1882–1958) One of Australia's greatest explorers, English-born Mawson was the geologist selected to join Ernest Shackleton's *Nimrod* expedition (1907–1909). As a member of the scientific team, he joined the ascent of Mount Erebus and the journey to the South Magnetic Pole. He went on to command the Australasian Antarctic Expedition, 1911–1914, in the *Aurora*. In 1912, Mawson was the sole survivor against the odds of the Far Eastern Party, as he describes in his book *Home of the Blizzard*, first published in 1915. He was knighted in 1914 and led the British, Australian and New Zealand Antarctic Research Expedition (BANZARE) in the *Discovery* in 1929–1930 and 1930–1931.

Meares, Cecil (1877–1937) A traveller, adventurer and trader in the East, Meares was appointed by Scott in 1910 to buy dogs and ponies in Siberia and then transport them to New Zealand to join the *Terra Nova* expedition. He was the only experienced dog driver among the British team and persuaded Dimitri Gerov to join the expedition when buying the dogs.

Murray-Levick, George (1877–1956) Murray-Levick was senior surgeon on the *Terra Nova* expedition and one of the Northern Party that spent the winter of 1912 living in an ice cave when they became stranded. He also studied the Adélie penguin colonies at Cape Adare and his book *Antarctic Penguins* (1914) was the standard work on the subject for many years.

Nansen, Fridtjof (1861–1930) In 1893 Nansen, the Norwegian Arctic explorer and marine biologist, had sailed to the Arctic on board the specially designed *Fram*, hoping to drift across the North Pole. Although unable to reach his final destination, the expedition provided much new information about the Arctic Ocean, proving that sea surrounded the Pole. He published his account of the expedition in *Farthest North*, first published in English translation in 1897. He became an Ambassador for Norway and a respected polar authority, advising Scott, Amundsen and Shackleton alike.

Oates, Captain Lawrence Edward Grace (1880–1912) Known as 'Titus' or 'the Soldier', Oates was an expert horseman. In 1900 he joined the 6th Inniskilling Dragoons and served as a subaltern in the Boer War, where he received a serious bullet wound to his left thigh. The injury left him with a shortened leg and was to contribute to his death. On the basis of his skill with horses, Oates was put in charge of the ponies on the *Terra Nova* expedition, though he was not instructed to buy them. He also gave a substantial contribution of £1,000 towards the costs of the expedition, offering his services free. As one of Scott's final South Pole party he suffered particularly badly from malnutrition, frostbite and probably scurvy, affecting his leg wound. He is best remembered for his self-sacrifice in walking out of the tent to his certain death on the return journey on 17 March 1912. He is the only soldier to die in a non-combatant role who is commemorated by the Army.

Omelchenko, Anton Lukish (1883–1932) Born in Bat'ki, Russia, Omelchenko was groom on the *Terra Nova* expedition, assisting with the ponies.

Pennell, Harry LL (1882–1916) Pennell was navigator in the *Terra Nova*. A gifted amateur naturalist, he also helped Wilson in the study of birds during the early part of the expedition.

Ponting, Herbert George (1870–1935) Herbert Ponting was photographer and cinematographer on the *Terra Nova* expedition. Born in Salisbury, Ponting travelled to the United States, after a short interlude in banking, where he worked in ranching and mining before taking up photography in 1900. He travelled widely in the Far East, building a reputation for his work.

By 1909 he had an international name as a photographer and was appointed by Scott as 'camera artist' for the *Terra Nova* expedition. Known as 'Ponko', he was inspired by the light and landscape of Antarctica and his black-and-white work remains unequalled. During the dark winter nights, Ponting entertained the men with lantern-slide shows of his exploits in Japan and China.

As the first professional photographer to visit Antarctica, he created a dramatic and beautiful visual record of the early part of the expedition. Ponting was unable to gain permission from Scott to accompany the Southern Party on their push for the Pole, because it was impractical to transport his heavy equipment.

On his return to Britain he released the classic film *90° South* and wrote *The Great White South* (1921), illustrated with many of his photographs.

Royds, Charles W Rawson (1876–1931) Born in Rochdale, Charles Royds followed his family tradition and joined the Royal Navy serving initially as a cadet aboard HMS *Conway*. His application to join the *Discovery* expedition was accepted in 1899 and he served as first lieutenant, also making a remarkable journey east across the Ross Ice Shelf to conduct magnetic work. Cape Royds was named after him. Royds died as a vice-admiral, having also been knighted for his last role as an assistant commissioner of the Metropolitan Police.

Scott, Captain Robert Falcon (1868–1912)
See Chapter 2 (page 32), Chapter 4 (page 78) and Chapter 8 (page 174).

Shackleton, Sir Ernest Henry (1874–1922)
See Chapter 2 (page 32), Chapter 7 (page 148), and Chapter 8 (page 174).

Simpson, Dr George Clarke (1878–1965) Simpson was meteorologist on the *Terra Nova* expedition.

Wild, John Robert Francis (1873–1939) Known to all as 'Frank', Wild was born in Skelton, North Yorkshire. He spent 11 years in the merchant navy before joining the Royal Navy in 1900. He was chosen from some 3,000 naval applicants to join the *Discovery*. Wild was later selected by Shackleton to serve on the *Nimrod* expedition and was a member of the party to reach its furthest point south at latitude 82° 23'. He was leader of the western base party on Douglas Mawson's Australasian Antarctic Expedition of 1911–1914 in the *Aurora*. His brother, Ernest Wild, was a surviving member of the ill-fated Ross Sea Party on the Imperial Trans-Antarctic Expedition, in which three men died. With such extensive Antarctic experience, and being a warm admirer of Shackleton, he was an automatic choice as second-in-command for the *Endurance* expedition. He remained in command of the men on Elephant Island while they awaited rescue. He went on to sail with Shackleton on his final voyage in the *Quest*.

Wilson, Dr Edward Adrian (1872–1912) Wilson was assistant surgeon on the *Discovery* expedition. A deeply religious man, he was also a skilled artist and his drawings, sketches and paintings present an evocative view of the Antarctic landscape. Wilson's sympathetic character soon marked him out as a key figure in maintaining team spirit and morale. Scott relied heavily on him for advice, guidance and moral support. He joined the *Terra Nova* as scientific director and zoologist, responsible for the management and welfare of the scientific research team on the expedition. His selfless character earned him the nickname 'Uncle Bill'. Wilson was automatically a member of the final South Pole party and died alongside Scott and Bowers on the return journey from the Pole.

Worsley, Frank Arthur (1872–1943) Born at Akaroa, New Zealand, Frank Worsley served as a reserve officer in the Royal Navy, 1904–1914, before becoming master of the *Endurance* in 1914. His navigation and seamanship on the 800-mile voyage of the *James Caird* to South Georgia was outstanding. He served on two ships in the First World War and was awarded the DSO and CBE. He sailed with Shackleton again in the *Quest* in 1921.

BIBLIOGRAPHY

and suggested further reading

Alexander, Caroline, *The 'Endurance': Shackleton's Legendary Antarctic Expedition*, London, Bloomsbury Publishing (1999).

Amundsen, Roald, *Sydpolen (The South Pole)*, Norway, Jacob Dybwabs Forlag (1912).

Arnold, HJP , *Photographer of the World: the Biography of Herbert Ponting*, London, Hutchinson (1969).

Bainbridge, Beryl, *The Birthday Boys*, London, Gerald Duckworth & Co. Ltd (1991).

Barnes, John, *Pioneers of the British Film*, London, Bishopsgate Press (1983).

Bickel, Lennard, *In Search of Frank Hurley*, London, Macmillan (1980).

Bickel, Lennard, *Shackleton's Forgotten Men*, Boston, Da Capo Press (2001).

Borchgrevink, C E, *First on the Antarctic Continent*, London, George Newnes (1901).

Bryan, Rorke, *Ordeal by Ice: Ships of the Antarctic*, New York, Sheridan House (2011).

Brownlow, Kevin, *The War, the West and the Wilderness*, London, Secker & Warburg (1979).

Cherry-Garrard, Apsley, *The Worst Journey in the World*, London, Carroll & Graf (1922).

Feeney, Robert E, *Polar Journeys: the role of food and nutrition in early exploration*, Alaska, University of Alaska Press (1998).

Fiennes, Sir Ranulph, *To the Ends of the Earth*, North Carolina, McNally & Loftin Publishers (1983).

Fiennes, Sir Ranulph, *Mind over Matter*, London, Sinclair-Stevenson Ltd (1993).

Fiennes, Sir Ranulph, *Captain Scott*, London, Hodder & Stoughton (2003).

Foreign and Commonwealth Office/British Antarctic Survey, *Antarctica (Schools Pack)*, London (1999).

Fuchs, Sir Vivian and Hillary, Sir Edmund, *The Crossing of Antarctica*, London, Cassell (1958).

Fuchs, Sir Vivian, *Of Ice and Men*, Shrewsbury, Anthony Nelson (1982).

Fuchs, Sir Vivian, *A Time to Speak*, Shrewsbury, Anthony Nelson (1990).

Gran, Tryggve, *The Norwegian with Scott*, London, Stationery Office Books (1984).

Hempleman-Adams, David, *Toughing it Out*, London, Orion Books (1998).

Hempleman-Adams, David, *Walking on Thin Ice*, London, Orion Books (1999).

Huntford, Roland, *Shackleton*, London, Hodder & Stoughton (1985).

Huntford, Roland, *Scott and Amundsen* [republished as *The Last Place on Earth*], London, Hodder & Stoughton (1979).

Huntford, Roland, *The Amundsen Photographs*, London, Hodder & Stoughton (1987).

Hurley, Frank, *Argonauts of the South*, New York, G. P. Putnam's Sons (1925).

Huxley, Elspeth, *Scott of the Antarctic*, New York, Atheneum Books (1977).

Jarvis, Tim, S*hackleton's Epic: Recreating the World's Greatest Journey of Survival*, London, William Collins (2013).

Larsen, Edward J, *An Empire of Ice: Scott, Shackleton, and the Heroic Age of Antarctic Science*, New Haven, Yale University Press (2011).

Limb, S and Cordingley, P, *Captain Oates: Soldier and Explorer*, London, B. T. Batsford (1982).

Locke, Stephen, *George Marston: Shackleton's Antarctic Artist*, Hampshire, Hampshire County Council (2000).

Mawson, Sir Douglas, *The Home of the Blizzard*, London, William Heinemann (1915).

Mills, Leif, *Frank Wild*, Whitby, Caedmon of Whitby (1999).

Ponting, Herbert, *The Great White South*, London, Duckworth & Co. (1921).

Preston, Diana, *A First Rate Tragedy: Captain Scott's Antarctic Expeditions*, London, Constable & Robinson (1997).

Riffenburgh, Beau, *Nimrod: Ernest Shackleton and the extraordinary story of the 1907–09 British Arctic Expedition*, London, Bloomsbury Publishing (2004).

Riffenburgh, Beau and Cruwys, Liz, *The Photographs of H. G. Ponting*, Discovery Gallery (1998).

Savours, Ann, *Scott's Last Voyage: through the Antarctic Camera of Herbert Ponting*, London, Sidgwick & Jackson Ltd (1974).

Savours, Ann, *The Voyages of the 'Discovery': The Illustrated History of Scott's Ship*, London, Virgin Books (1992).

Scott, RF *The Voyage of the 'Discovery'*, London, John Murray (1905).

Scott, RF (ed Huxley, Leonard), *Scott's Last Expedition*, New York, Dodd, Mead and Company (1913).

Shackleton, Sir Ernest, *Aurora Australis*, privately published (1908).

Shackleton, Sir Ernest, *The Heart of the Antarctic*, London, William Heinemann (1909).

Shackleton, Sir Ernest, *South*, London, Century Publishing (1919).

Solomon, Susan, *The Coldest March. Scott's Fatal Antarctic Expedition*, New Haven, Yale University Press (2001).

Spufford, Francis, *I may be some time: Ice and the English Imagination*, London, Faber & Faber (1996).

Stroud, Mike, *Shadows on the Wasteland*, New York, Overlook Books (1994).

Thomas, Lowell, *Sir Hubert Wilkins: His World of Adventure*, New York, McGraw-Hill (1961).

Tyler-Lewis, Kelly, *The Lost Men. The Harrowing Story of Shackleton's Ross Sea Party*, London, Bloomsbury Publishing (2006).

Wheeler, Sara, *Cherry: A Life of Apsley Cherry-Garrard*, London, Vintage/Ebury (2002).

Wheeler, Sara, *Terra Incognita*, London, Vintage (1997).

Wilson, EA (ed. Savours, Ann), *The Diary of the 'Discovery' Expedition to the Antarctic Regions* (1901–1904), London, Blandford Press (1966).

Worsley, Frank A, *Shackleton's Boat Journey*, London, Hodder & Stoughton (1940).

Recommended websites

Antarctic Co-operative Research Centre, www.acecrc.org.au

Antarctic Philately, www.south-pole.com

Australian Antarctic Division, www.antarctica.gov.au

British Antarctic Survey, www.bas.ac.uk

Byrd Polar Research Center, https://bpcrc.osu.edu

Cheltenham Art Gallery and Museum, www.cheltenhammuseum.org.uk

Council of Managers of National Antarctic Programs, www.comnap.aq

Discovery Point, www.rrsdiscovery.com

Edinburgh University Library, www.ed.ac.uk/information-services/library-museum-gallery

Engineering Electronic Library, Sweden (EELS), http://vlib.ustuarchive.urfu.ru/storon/ellib_sveden/index.html

Endurance, wwwde.kodak.com/US/en/corp/features/endurance/home/index.shtml

National Library of Scotland, www.nls.uk

National Maritime Museum, Greenwich, London, www.rmg.co.uk

Natural Environment Research Council, www.nerc.ac.uk

Norwegian Polar Institute, www.npolar.no/en

Office of Polar Programs at the National Science Foundation, www.nsf.gov/div/index.jsp?div=OPP

Royal Geographic Society, www.rgs.org

Scientific Committee on Antarctic Research, www.scar.org

Scott Polar Research Institute, University of Cambridge, www.spri.cam.ac.uk

Shackleton's Antarctic Odyssey, https://www.pbs.org/wgbh/nova/shackletonexped

Shetland Museum, www.shetland-museum.org.uk

West Antarctic Ice Sheet Initiative, www.waisworkshop.org

INDEX

PICTURE CREDITS

We are grateful to the following for permission to reproduce images:

National Maritime Museum, Greenwich, London
16 PAH8482; 18 G266:1/7; 21 PAJ1628; 22 G201:3/1(2); 25 PAF0588;
26 PAD6215; 27 AAA0943; 29 ALB1396.2; 29 ALB1396.2; 34 PAG6631;
36 P49376; 39 C7267/B; 40 C4269B; 40 ALB0346.16; 41 ALB0346.12;
42 PBF1103/1; 43 PBB4147; 44 ALB0346.34; 45 ALB0346.36;
45 ALB0346.40; 48 P49449; 48 P49447; 48 ALB1396.168;
50 RSS/MC/FAMOUSINDIVIDUALS; 52 AML/Z/18(2); 54 P49379;
61 MED0481; 64 P49378; 66 ILN/1903/123; 70 PBB4110; 89 ALB1217.1;
93 ALB1217.34; 93 ALB1217.40; 94 ALB1217.6; 98 ALB1217.36;
99 ALB1217.32; 113 AAA4171; 126 ZBA1615.6; 138 ZBA1691; 148 P11;
151 P15; 154 P4; 158 P14; 160 P12; 161 AAB0225; 166 AAA3415;
166 AAA3418; 169 ZBA1610; 172 P5600; 173 ZBA2271; 178 ALB1401.39;
180 ALB1401.35; 181 ALB1401.41; 184 AAA4270

**National Maritime Museum, Greenwich, London, Greenwich
Hospital Collection**
20 BHC2628

National Maritime Museum, Caird Fund
24 BHC2981; National Maritime Museum, Greenwich, London, Tizard
Collection; 26 ALB0859.40

**National Maritime Museum, Greenwich, London. Acquired with
assistance from the Heritage Lottery Fund**
90 ZBA1609; 113 ZBA1612; 113 ZBA1613

Getty Images
2 Herbert Ponting/Scott Polar Research Institute, University of
Cambridge/Getty Images; 6 Captain Robert Falcon Scott/Popperfoto/
Getty Images; 10 Captain Robert Falcon Scott/Popperfoto/Getty
Images; 12 Photo by Mario Tama/Getty Images; 31 Herbert Ponting/
Scott Polar Research Institute, University of Cambridge/Getty
Images; 33 John Thomson/Hulton Archive/Getty Images; 58 Hulton
Archive/Getty Images; 61 Spencer Arnold/Getty Images; 83 Print
Collector/Getty Images; 91 Herbert Ponting/Scott Polar Research
Institute, University of Cambridge/Getty Images; 94 Historical
Picture Archive/CORBIS/Corbis via Getty Images; 100 Captain
Robert Falcon Scott/Popperfoto/Getty Images; 106 Bob Thomas/
Popperfoto/Getty Images; 108 Popperfoto/Getty Images;
109 Bettmann/Getty Images; 114 Popperfoto/Getty Images;
117 Popperfoto/Getty Images; 118 Ben Stansall/AFP/Getty Images;
119 Popperfoto/Getty Images; 122 Antarctic Heritage Trust/ Barcroft
India /Barcoft Media via Getty Images; 125 Frank Hurley/Scott Polar
Research Institute, University of Cambridge/Getty Images; 128
Popperfoto/Getty Images; 132 Frank Hurley/Scott Polar Research
Institute, University of Cambridge/Getty Images; 135 Topical Press
Agency/Getty Images; 136 SSPL/Getty Images; 137 Bob Thomas/
Popperfoto/Getty Images; 139 Frank Hurley/Scott Polar Research
Institute, University of Cambridge/Getty Images; 142 Popperfoto/
Getty Images; 174 Herbert Ponting/Scott Polar Research Institute,
University of Cambridge/Getty Images; 177 Hulton-Deutsch
Collection/CORBIS/Corbis via Getty Images; 177 Bettmann/Getty
Images; 183 Wolfgang Kaehler/LightRocket via Getty Images

Other sources
27 Courtesy of Gerlache family archives; 56 North Wind Picture
Archives / Alamy Stock Photo; 67 Bill Douglas Museum; 72 National
Library of New Zealand; 74 Mirror Archives; 80, 85, 86, 87 Fram
Museum, Oslo; 81, 105 National Library of Norway; 113 Scott Polar
Research Institute, University of Cambridge; 115, 116 Wellcome
Collection; 165 Dulwich College; 178 Joyce Collection, Canterbury
Museum, New Zealand